RADICAL WOMAN

RESILIENCE AFTER DIFFICULT ISSUES, CHANGES AND LOSSES

This book was compiled by visionary:

International Best-Selling Author, Ayanna Mills Ambrose, M.B.A.

Authors: Beatrice Charles, Blanca Solorzano, Dr. Anu Binny,

Dr. Margarita David, Dr. Merary Simeon, Erica Nobles, Felicia Butler,

Katina Walker, Orjanette Bryant, Rickkita Edwards, Tammy Lyons,

Tarsha Howard, Teresa Moreno, and Tonya Kent

Foreword by: Dr. Sheka Houston

DISCLAIMER

Disclaimer: Any information, characters, and events within the compilation of stories or other related and linked materials are the sole opinion of each individual author and only for entertainment. The views expressed have no relation to those of any academic, hospital, office practice, or corporate institutions with which the authors are affiliated. Neither the lead author nor co-authors are dispensing medical or legal advice. They do not intend any of this information to be used for self-diagnosis, treatment, or legal strategy. Never disregard professional, medical or legal advice or delay in seeking it because of something you have read in this book or any related and linked materials.

If you think you may have a medical emergency, then call your doctor or emergency room immediately. To the maximum extent permitted by law, the author, related entities, and the publisher disclaim all responsibility and liability to any person, arising directly or indirectly from any person acting or not acting based on the information provided.

TABLE OF CONTENTS

ACKNOWLEDGMENTS

I give honor to God from whom all my blessings flow. To each author who shared their story to contribute to such an ambitious and worthy project: I am in awe of your accomplishments, determination, and strength. Your stories are powerful beyond measure, and I have no doubt they will inspire many women to find the courage to bounce back after facing difficult issues, changes, and losses.

To Dr. Sheka Houston: My eternal gratitude for your far-reaching vision, inspirational leadership, and endless encouragement.

To our editor, Tamika Sims: Thank you for helping us polish our testimonies so that we may share them with the world.

Finally, a heartfelt thanks to our special loved ones, near and far, who are our biggest cheerleaders and selfless supporters in all our endeavors. Your support has contributed to our fight to become radical women, and we are forever grateful.

DEDICATION

This book is dedicated to anyone who has been abused, rejected, abandoned and left to pick up the pieces. We want you to know that it is normal to deal with hard times, but you were created to win and live a satisfying life.

"For I know the plans I have for you," says the Lord. "They are plans for good and not for disaster, to give you a future and a hope."

Jeremiah 29:11 NLT

This book is also dedicated to everyone struggling with the adverse effects of the Coronavirus. We pray that our stories will inspire you to keep going because trouble doesn't last forever.

"For I reckon that the sufferings of this present time are not worthy to be compared with the glory which shall be revealed in us."

Romans 8:18 KJV

FOREWORD

Dr. Sheka Houston

I s it better to go through life's struggles alone and when it's over to act like the problem never existed? Is it better to seek wise counsel, conquer challenges, and give others hope to do the same thing? I prefer the latter.

According to government entities, there are several adverse effects of abuse on women's health to include heart problems, high blood pressure, and digestive problems. Women who are abused are also more likely to develop depression, anxiety, or eating disorders and may also misuse alcohol or drugs as a means to cope. The Department of Justice has found that 84%-86% of abuse victims are women.

Many times, abuse can lead to divorce, which can impact all involved negatively. Abuse of power is deeply rooted in abuse but can also be found in the practices of unfair discrimination, which could be invoked by a narcissistic person. According to equal rights organizations, 42% of women in the workplace have experienced discrimination. Consequently, this book and what the authors have come together to do is so important. I believe that reading this book will help some to overcome obstacles and others to start the healing process.

Create and Educate

My name is Dr. Sheka Houston, and I am a middle school principal and business owner. I entered education to allow students the opportunity to see more positive role models because that is what impacted me as a student. I have 18 years of experience in public schools and recently added bestselling author, trainer, and coach as the co-founder of Create and Educate, LLC. I help provide equity and access for small businesses, such as authors and speakers, to become vendors in schools. I work to bring people together to collaborate for great causes to benefit children and businesses.

I met Ayanna Mills Ambrose (Gallow) during a virtual Christmas event sponsored by my company that we held to encourage children to continue reading during a school break because promoting literacy is one of our greatest passions. As a featured author, she did an incredible job of connecting with our audience. Ayanna's personal story is so triumphant and inspiring, and her mission is admirable. Helping other women experience this same triumph through her anthology work and even propelling them to success as bestselling authors are influential. Truly meaningful work that aligns with my belief in the power of collaboration.

Radical Woman: Resilience After Difficult Issues, Changes and Losses

In this book, these talented ladies discuss their personal struggles with various issues on difficult issues, changes, and losses. Having a mother who overcame dyslexia, having experienced unfair treatment, and growing up as a child who was a product of divorce, I know personally what it's like to overcome adversity. As a wife, mother, and educator, I know how important it is for others to hear these stories so they will know what is possible and what could be. There is excellent work surrounding this message in education, and this is why representation on so many levels are so important.

In this book, the authors also discuss how they overcame their respective tragedies. These ladies are to be commended for their strength, boldness, and care for humankind that exists in them to ensure the things that happened to them can be prevented from happening to others. These stories can change someone else's story. This is to be celebrated!

Congratulations to each of the phenomenal authors featured in *Radical Woman: Resilience After Difficult Issues, Changes and Losses*! You all have hoped, believed, and triumphed. Now you inspire. Your journey has been purposeful, and I applaud you for hearing and obeying the call for this work because it is essential and life-changing. I also applaud the work and vision of Ayanna Mills Ambrose, who continues to help so many find their voices and become victors. I extend my most genuine congratulations to each of you for such a tremendous and worthwhile accomplishment. In words inspired by a great quote from Frederick Douglass, my hopes were never brighter than they are right now. Continue to rise above all adversities. Continue to inspire. Continue to soar. It matters.

Dr. Sheka Houston

INTRODUCTION

Ayanna Mills Ambrose

I s it our scariest days or our last days? Do we have the faith to make it, or is the pain beyond repair? If we develop resilience, then we will not only outlast today's painful realities but also embark on the beauty of tomorrow.

I am Ayanna Mills Ambrose, and I am the visionary author of *Radical Woman: Resilience After Difficult Issues, Changes and Losses*. I live in a beautiful home, I have a great relationship with my parents, and I am happily married to my high-school sweetheart. Thus, I am happy with my life. The other side to my story is, I grew up in a packed house that was raided by the police for drugs, I was conceived in rape and born six weeks after my mother's 13th birthday, and I was abandoned in my first marriage. Yet, if I had the option to go through my painful past to be where I am today, then I would embrace the pain.

"Different Strokes"

There are two sides to every coin. Although each side looks different, both sides make up one coin, and the value is not determined based on which side the coin is on. Comparatively, there are two sides to every story. No matter what side of life a person is in, their worth is not diminished based on their current circumstances. Many people face tragedies, but they only share one side of their story to avoid being perceived as different from everyone else. However, I need to show both sides not only for my own progression but also to let others know that it was my pain that birthed my purpose.

"And they overcame him by the blood of the Lamb,
and by the word of their testimony. (Revelation 12:11 KJV)

The purpose of this book is to provide transparency to real-life struggles. This book discusses 15 women's successful outcomes following educational and financial challenges, difficult issues resulting from trauma, and painful losses - to empower other women.

"*The Facts of Life*"

According to the CDC, women are more likely to experience child sexual abuse and sexual assault. Also, 10 of every 100 women (or 10%) develop PTSD sometime in their lives compared with about 4 of every 100 men (or 4%). Therefore, from childhood to adulthood, women deal with trauma.

Although so many women face trauma, they conceal their pain due to shame, which leads to negative emotions. I know this well because I wore a mask of happiness for a long time. Allow me to introduce my transformational story and the origin of this book.

"*Growing Pains*"

I am amongst the 1% of people conceived in rape. My mother's stepfather raped her at 12, which resulted in my birth when she was 13. If you think that sounds bad, let me add to that by saying that my grandmother allowed her rapist husband to remain in the home, and I grew up in the house with both of my parents. Traumatic, to say the least.

"*Family Ties*"

My pain came from my family dynamics. I was embarrassed by my alcoholic father/step-grandfather, and I had to watch him succumb to cirrhosis of the liver. I was confused as to why my grandmother let him remain in the home after he raped my mother/her daughter. I was also scared for my mother due to the aching look she displayed every time others learned we were only 13 years apart. Most painfully, I was devastated for myself because I could never change the fact that the blood running through my body came from a rapist. I chose to remain silent regarding my feelings. As a result, I suffered internal pain, and I suffered alone.

I went from being a silent child to a published author. To overcome my childhood trauma emotions and find my voice as an author, I had to start with recognizing that I could not change the past, who was wrong, or who was at fault; I had to take charge to focus on my future. The keys to my success were:

G- Goals: I watched sitcoms that displayed good family dynamics and emphasized college. This helped me to visualize what my life could be. Thus, I set goals to create the life I wanted.

O-Optimism: Despite the malignant tension at home between my mother and father, my mother made sure to boost my self-image by telling me things like "my brain was like a computer." When she said that to me, I believed her, it made me think I could learn and do anything. Therefore, I believed in myself and always aimed high.

D-Determination: I was determined to become successful. I would let positive affirmations, like my brain, which is like a computer, fuel my determination for learning. I gave 100% to education and academics. I had perfect attendance from elementary through high school. In high school, I was inducted into the National Honor Society, and I graduated college Magna Cum Laude from the honors program. The determination for success led me to always be the top producer in my field, which enabled me to exceed my financial goals. It also led me to use my voice to help others, so I started writing, which led me to become an author.

In 2019, I wrote and published a book titled *God & Hip Hop: A 21 Day Biblical Devotional Inspired by Hip Hop.* In this devotional, I revealed the story of my birth. After the book was released, it shocked many people to learn that I suffered in silence because they only saw the side I wanted them to see, but now I was showing both sides.

People began confiding in me about their struggles because they felt freer after reading mine. Seeing the positive impact of one story made me want to produce more. I wanted to help people focus on goals, optimism, and determination (God), so that they could heal internal pain (HIP) and have happiness, opportunities, and prosperity (HOP). Therefore, I began compiling transformational non-fiction stories, and you are about to embark on my latest one.

Radical Woman: Resilience After Difficult Issues, Changes and Losses

In this book, the authors discuss their road to success to empower women to flip the coin if they do not like the side it's on. This book comprises transformational stories on overcoming abuse, divorce, dyslexia, low self-esteem, narcissism, poverty, and unfair treatment. Through the transformational stories shared, we hope this book will prevent young women from making common mistakes, motivate women in the middle of a mess, and encourage all women to dream.

Dream

Dream with determination

Dream without limitation

Dream with high expectation

Dream in spite of your situation

Dream and become an inspiration

Dream and help others reach their destination

Dream until you see your manifestation

Dream

Ayanna Ambrose

Empowerment
For Education &
Financial Improvement

"Great things come from hard work and perseverance. No excuses."- Kobe Bryant

Abandonment to Self-made

Dr. Anu Binny

I have braved abandonment twice. Once on a somber afternoon in October 1972 as a weeny third child of an orthodox Indian family that was unprepared to bring home a girl. The second time was in April 2015, as a scarred married lady of a patriarchal family that was not ready to accept a woman who chose to regain her authentic self.

It was mid-April 2015 when I found myself with two bedsheets bundled with everyday clothes, some certificates, and both children on either side. I ran away from everything I had come to identify myself with and given almost half of my life to. But I also left behind an abusive relationship, fear, and anxiety. I had not a penny to my name and chose to make the sacrifice of leaving a home and everything I had worked hard for, to make a brand-new beginning.

Domestic violence happens to people from all walks of life. Alarming statistics indicate that in developed countries, a woman becomes the victim of physical assault approximately every nine seconds! Developing countries will have more staggering figures. According to The National Centre on Family Homelessness, Domestic Violence is among the top five leading causes of homelessness. Paradoxically, the fear of homelessness, is also one of the primary reasons why women continue to suffer and stay with the abuser.

I too chose to be silent for many years. But I can't be silent anymore. I am here to tell my story in the hope that it will help you believe in the power of your voice, your choices, and that you can achieve success and recognition even when the going gets impossibly tough.

Bumping into the limits and breaking free

The glitter of luminaries and dazzle of the electrifying crowd filled me with excitement. I was here at the award-winning event where I had been nominated for the India HR Future leader award that would be flashed across the leading business newspaper in India. I had also recently earned a doctorate in Engineering that allowed me to add "Dr." to my name.

From the stage, I could see my daughter beaming at me with pride. She had taken a day off from attending Engineering college to be with me at the award function. "*You made it Mumma!*" she laughed, happy tears rolling down her cheeks, as she hugged me tightly. I too locked myself in her embrace, holding the award tightly, and feeling immensely grateful to God that I had made it this far.

It had not been an easy journey and God knows I tried. Thoughts drifted to a couple of months ago when I fell hard on the floor, hurled with a slap that demanded me to sign a check. My ex-husband was a controlling, manipulative man and I often felt browbeaten into doing things I didn't want to. He had coerced and arm-twisted me into transferring my earlier salaries to him. I was refusing to do it for this month. I wanted to send my extremely introverted daughter to a leadership program. This led to a heated argument. I could see my daughter's shadow quietly walking towards the commotion. I sprung up from the floor to save her from the fateful sight. Our eyes met briefly, and she disappeared into her room, crying.

This made me livid. This time I was determined to not give in and demanded to know what had happened to all the money I had earned. "*I don't know. You should know, after all, it is in your bank account.*" He replied nonchalantly. I reminded him that it was he who was always in control of the money and had assured me that he had set aside money for the kid's education.

When I started asking questions, I was hurled with a slap to be silenced. The older women of his family looked on unemotionally as she told me to lower my voice when I cried out aloud with throbbing pain. This was not the first time. Today it was about money. The reasons changed with circumstances but staying quiet had been my only option.

This time I refused to give in. So, the exchange of words continued, finally concluding that I was not a good wife. I was not submissive, and finally nose-diving into talking about the one and only childhood puppy love story that I had shared with him. For a moment, I stood there aghast. The stories I once whispered during private, intimate moments, were now weaponized.

I stared at him in disbelief, shocked at the way the context got twisted and I was being labeled a slutty woman. "*If I had known that you were such a petty penny, I would have never married you,*" he yelled at me. I turned and with all the voice I could garner replied, "*Watch out, for you have only this penny with you today and tomorrow you will not have even that.*" I picked up my bag, left for work amidst tears, threats, and accusations.

I finished my day's work and was totally exhausted. My job was demanding, and I had a new boss too. I closed my laptop, finally opening my mind again to the entire painful experience I had that morning. I wondered at the years that had gone by. I had to walk on eggshells every day because I was fearful of speaking my mind. I had thought of walking away multiple times but eventually stayed on because of early pregnancy, my shattered self-esteem, and lack of support. I needed a roof over my head and a safe place for my children and slowly came to believe that I deserved to be treated poorly. The frequent bruises were hidden under clothing or masked under makeup. Over the years, I watched my self-identity dissolve like salt in water.

It was late when I rang the bell. I could see that dinner had been served and everybody was eating. Life seemed to be back to normal. For the first time, I realized that what I was going through didn't matter to anyone.

I felt hurt and embarrassed and yet I still questioned whether I was making too much of it? But imagine my surprise when my then 16-year-old daughter after dinner, sat me down and said, *"Mumma, I have to say this to you today. He is never going to change. No matter how many times you pretend nothing happened and make excuses, he is never, ever going to change. You need to decide if that's how you want to spend the rest of your life."* Such clarity of thought and vocal support from my 16-year-old gave me the strength I was looking for.

My son who was too young to understand what was going on shared his usual 'what happened in school chatter' and tried to make me laugh with his funny quips. I tucked him to bed and retired to my room. That night, I slept facing away from him. I struggled with one decision: stay or leave. *"I have kept the bank check on the dining table, don't forget to sign it before you leave for work tomorrow morning,"* he warned before switching off the lights. With tears on my pillow, I reflected on my journey. Having been raised in a nuclear family, I had always longed for large close-knit families and thought I was lucky when I got married into a joint family.

I loved the idea of living with a family that had elders around. Just like most of the girls in a small town in India, I grew up in a culture that constantly reminded me that girls did not belong to the family they were born but to the one they were married into. 'Study hard, get a job, and marry a boy your parents choose.' This was the mantra that was drilled into my consciousness since childhood. And that is what I did. But nobody told me about getting beaten, nobody talked about abuse, or manipulation. Those I had to figure out by myself.

21

I had been taught to always put others before myself because good women silently bore everything, hid their pain, and never complained. I had reached out to my parents a couple of times earlier, but they had always said that things would change someday. They asked me to trust God, pray harder, and wait for my miracle. My brothers too agreed to the same. 'Suffering is the destiny of every woman,' my mother's voice echoed in my ears.

His mother expressed the same views in action in a thousand subtle ways, that I was not good enough for her son or for her family. I had shared my woes with his closest relative, but she expressed surprise that I felt like that and said- "Isn't it your job to keep my brother happy?" Perhaps they were blinded by their own upbringing and the skewed ways the patriarchal society worked. But no good came of it to me. Over the years, I had resigned to being a meek, inanimate object around my own house.

I wondered if I had stayed on for too long, especially because I knew that I was all alone. When I looked back, I saw that I had allowed everybody else around me to make decisions and steer my life in the direction of their choice and I had become a doormat. But this time it was different. It was about my children and their future. I finally implored my parents to come and get me out of this hellhole. They hesitated because of the social stigma around bringing back a married daughter, with her children at that! After a month and a half, they finally came around but asked me to look for a place somewhere in Mumbai where I could start afresh. It broke my heart to put my teenage kids through this.

Separation before divorce is an emotional roller coaster. Divorce is, in fact, akin to bereavement, so I went through all the stages before coming to accept the loss. I felt shocked, disbelief, anger, and guilt. Losing my marriage left me feeling like I had permanently and irrevocably failed at the single most important thing in my life. But accepting my situation and realizing that I can claim my life back, helped me build my confidence, and trust myself more than anybody else.

I decided that it was time I came out of hiding and reached out for help and comfort. It dawned on me that I had not made one new friend in decades. I talked to all the people that I had lived and grown up with. It was a rude shock to find that none of them would stand by me. Perhaps they were justified in thinking I had abandoned them in the first place. I had been so busy running the house and trying hard to fit into a one-size-fits-all garment of a docile Indian bride, that I barely had time to live for myself, let alone stay in touch with friends.

I had so much to do. My life ahead seemed suddenly barren and plain. But I told myself to look at the brighter side. I now had the freedom to do what I wanted without a worry in the world. I can go about filling my life with positive, happy, and nourishing elements even if that meant I was starting from scratch. I only bought the bare necessities, paid school fees, and set up a home that didn't make my kids feel 'poor.' I remember my son asking me if we might have to move to the slums. Finding happiness and working towards a beautiful dawn, was all I asked. The days were a blur of travel, work, home-keeping, and parenting. The nights I spent crying my heart out, getting the pain, hurt, and betrayal out of my system so I can begin the process of healing.

When you've been through hell, most people around you are only looking for juicy bits of gossip or live off of your misery. Sifting through the spite, hate, and rudeness that comes your way, even a neutral comment seems comforting. Patriarchy reeked through most comments and advice. Why didn't you keep your husband happy? Why couldn't you support the man of the house? He's such a nice guy! Why did you show off that you're more educated than him?

I was exhausted and tired of explaining my stance to unwilling ears. It took me several months, but I slowly realized that I must start seeing myself through my eyes, not through those of others.

I was glad to be an introvert which worked like magic for me. I kept my head low, withdrew myself from what little public life I allowed myself to indulge in, and channeled all of my energies into building a future that I would be proud of. At the center of my Universe were three people, my children and me.

Reinventing Me

I decided to handle emotions by writing to myself, meditating, praying, and swirling myself in a world of affirmations. I decided to use all my energies designing my life and carving my own path when I could see none. I decided to take it one day at a time.

The first step was to tear down the web of deception, especially fear.

The next was to undo my belief that I could not make the right decisions. Now, I allowed myself to make mistakes. I gathered all my fears and one-by-one, like a sculptor with a chisel, I went at them, undoing the wrong, and rediscovering myself.

I was opening up to the idea of making some brand-new relationships. I found strangers extremely helpful. I drew strength, hope, and inspiration from positive people around me.

Long hours of work, determination, and grit paved the way for awards and achievements. My kids started rebuilding their lives. Today, I am a proud Mumma as I watch both of them pursue their engineering degrees and have turned out to be fine human beings. Life has changed for the better.

I set a few aspirational goals and began investing in myself. I achieved most of them. I climbed up the corporate ladder and fulfilled my dream to become an entrepreneur. Today, I hold a doctorate in Engineering, I am an International Trainer, TEDx Speaker, and a Life coach. I help people succeed by designing their life, overcome life or career transitions or even failure to thrive financially, and live a life of freedom.

Rising Above

I was able to overcome the fear of abandonment, being judged, and the social disgrace of being a divorcee because it is not in the fall but when we *rise* that determines our destiny.

From the lady who chose to leave the rocky world of wrong choices, to flounder in the unfamiliar space of truth, to the one that rose like a phoenix from the ashes of a dark and bitter past, I've come a long way and hope that by sharing my journey it will give you the strength and hope you might want when you're looking for some.

It is true when they say that every night must end and there has to be a pretty dawn, shades of crimson pouring vibrantly into a quickly changing canvas on the horizon. My dawn is here. Yours will be too.

M.O.R.E. because N.O. is Not an Option

Teresa Moreno

How many times have you heard this?

You will never achieve anything, it is a shame that you are so pretty.

Most teens struggle with identifying who they are, where they are, and how they fit in, especially during a period when so many changes are happening all at once. If you do not have the support at home or school, then you end up looking for it elsewhere, anywhere, or in something that makes you feel welcomed and accepted as you are. Sometimes those places, people or things help alleviate some of the pain or loneliness. Come along on this journey with me and read how the inner battle comes from within, and the path to overcoming lies in discovering who you are, accepting yourself, and returning to your roots.

My Roots

My parents migrated from Mexico and brought six children with them to the United States. I am the first generation of Americans in my family. I cannot even imagine the struggles and many obstacles that they had to endure while making that trek in pursuit of providing a better future and a life filled with opportunities for their children. In their country, they both had to abandon their studies. My dad was put to work to contribute financially to the family, and my mom had to help raise her brothers and sisters.

They were both raised as Catholics and wanted to instill those religious values, morals, and traditions in their children. Spanish was the primary language spoken at home and my first language. My childhood consisted of attending Church on Sundays, Bible Study on Wednesdays, giving to the less fortunate, and enjoying family time at the park or swimming at the local neighborhood pool. I spent the Summer days playing freeze tag, baseball, roller skating, and riding bikes until the streetlights came on. As a kid, I was oblivious to the dangers that were lurking all around me.

Her Story

I was born in East Los Angeles and raised on the South-Central side. The neighborhood streets were riddled with gangs, crack-houses, drug dealers, murders, and drive-by shootings. In an effort to shield and guide us away from the streets, my parents made every sacrifice and effort for all of us to get a Catholic education. And so, I spent the first eight years of my academic life attending a Catholic school. My parents had little academic education. My dad had completed the fourth grade, my mom started but never completed first grade. Without reading or writing skills, she would struggle to sign her name using only her initials.

My parent's inability to speak, write or read English and their struggle to comprehend moved me to become their translator and interpreter for everything from tax, government, medical, and school forms at nine years old. My dad had many health issues, and I wanted to take care of him and my family. I knew this would be difficult since he had already had his right leg amputated. He lost his leg and his job. Despite the constant health challenges, he managed to continue on and eventually he would open his own business. By the time I was in junior high, my dad's health had deteriorated. He had been through multiple surgeries, dialysis and was in and out of hospitals, rehab centers, and convalescent homes.

In the Fall, my dad became ill, had been hospitalized and had more surgeries due to his complications with Diabetes. I started working a part-time job to support myself and lessen the burden on my mom. I spent many days alone, without supervision or care, since my mom would seek refuge in the church and their activities to keep her sane and get spiritual support to deal with my dad's illness, us kids, and our growing pains. There was no supervision at home, and eventually I found refuge in the streets with my cousins and friends.

After years of suffering from complications with Diabetes, my dad passed away one November. I was 15-years-old. My mom was never home, and I was on my own and would have to work even harder to achieve what I wanted. I managed to complete the ninth grade. I started at Chatsworth High in the San Fernando Valley, then transferred to Locke High School in the Watts neighborhood of the South L.A. region. Well known for its violence and low-test scores, it was one of the worst schools in LAUSD at the time. I saw kids with knives, guns, and teachers in fear for their life; heck, I was in fear for my life.

With problems at school and home with my mom, I stopped attending school to find full-time employment. I still wanted to continue my education and enrolled in a continuation school to complete my tenth-grade credits. I never finished those credits and would not be able to attend college. An article in the *Los Angeles Times*, stated that *"In the giant Los Angeles Unified School District, the dropout rate for the Class of 1990 was 40.9%..."* I became another statistic. I was officially a High School Dropout!

Mindset Shift

After I turned 16, I met a guy, quickly fell in love, and we became inseparable. We were both young and naïve about life and love. Having someone to care about me and give me attention made me feel special and wanted. I spent every moment I could with him and had separated myself from my friends because it would upset him when I would associate with them. At 18-years-old, I was giving birth to my first son. I was a teen mom, and that was the beginning of a vicious cycle known as Domestic Violence. I could not leave him. Our religious conviction was to stay with your husband and pray so that God will change him. The problems continued and I thought that a change of location would fix any issues we had.

We moved to Fresno, CA, and a few months later, my mom moved in with us to support me with my two kids now. I was dedicating myself to my kids and home and had participated in some network marketing companies with some success since it did not require a high school diploma. I always wanted to be a teacher and knew that it was not a possibility for me. Then one day my mom did something that shifted my belief and changed my mindset.

According to the *Washington Examiner*, 67% of Hispanic immigrants in the U.S. 15 years or more are functionally illiterate. My mom, at the age of 58, enrolled at the adult school to learn how to read and write. I was so inspired by her perseverance and excited to see her joy and elation with each new letter she learned to pronounce, read, and write. I was moved to fulfill my goal of attending college. But how? I did not have a high school diploma. I was scared and I went anyway to Fresno City College and asked for the application requirements. Since I didn't have a high school diploma, I would have to obtain my General Education Diploma (GED) or pass an ability to benefit test (ATB). If I passed the ATB, I would be able to attend without my GED.

At 23-years-old and with some tenth-grade education, I decided to take the ATB test, and I passed. I opted for an early childhood development degree. Later that year, I was offered a job at the local Head-start center as a Case Manager for the school year. By the end of the school year, my 3rd child was born in June, and my marriage was as rocky as it had been since the start.

Statistics have shown that a victim of domestic violence attempts to leave their abuser seven times before being successful. That was about the number of times it took me to finally leave and save myself and my children from the abuse. We had moved back to Los Angeles, and my children were now 7, 3, and

1 year old. The last incident left me battered and bruised from my face, arms and legs with a bulging purple and bloodied bump on the inner side of my knee where he had smashed and broken a toy gun. The next day, I packed the car with my kids, whatever fit and left. I found temporary refuge with family members and at a women's shelter facility. The next three years that followed were some of the most challenging of my life.

I knew that to provide a better future for my kids, the path for me was to go to school, get good grades to get a good job, and make good money. I enrolled at the local college to pursue my Associate of Science degree and provide a better future for my kids. Juggling many plates had been a knack I had fully developed since I was young. I was enrolled in school full-time during the day, coached their little league baseball and basketball teams, and studied at night. Two years later, I was walking across the stage as a graduate from East Los Angeles College. Then, I applied and was accepted at California State University, Los Angeles. In 2007, two years after I started, I had completed all the requirements and walked across the stage as a graduate with a Bachelor of Arts degree in Social Work. This was a significant achievement for me, considering I dropped out of high school. Nonetheless, I achieved two college degrees in four years.

Upon graduation, I was ready to take on the world; I was not ready to take an office job that would tie me down and limit my time and earnings. I chose to forgo all typical hospital, social service agency, or school case manager J.O.B.s (just over broke). I wanted to control my time, money, and travel when I wanted to, and the only way to do that is by becoming a business owner. So, I did and partnered up to open my first retail business.

My Transformation

I went from dropping out of high school, becoming a teen mom, a victim of domestic violence, and a single parent to obtaining my bachelor's degree in social work, becoming a business owner, and a community empowerment leader. Although I had to overcome discrimination and lack of access to resources, I was determined to become successful because I wanted M.O.R.E. and N.O. is not an option for my children and other women like me.

M.O.R.E.N.O. - My Transformation Process from Teenage Drop Out to Entrepreneur

M.- Mom- What has driven me and given me the strength to continue has been my children and the example and principles that I want to impart in them. The challenges I have faced as a woman/minority are why I have embarked on entrepreneurial endeavors to provide opportunities to women and to ensure my children's success.

O.- Opinion- I decided that the only thoughts and opinions that mattered were my own. I stopped listening to negative beliefs and I surrounded myself with good influences. I learned that I was my most valuable real estate, so I guarded myself against negativity and invested in myself to create a huge return on investment. I surrounded myself with people that inspired, uplifted, and helped me up. I learned not to be afraid to ask for help.

R. ROMA- I brought to life ROMA, which stands for **R**adical and **O**riginal ideas with **M**astery and **A**ction, ROMA Business Services, Inc. is a center dedicated to providing various community service workshops Financial Literacy, Personal Growth and Development, and Team Building. ROMA also provides books, education, and resources to the community.

E. Education- I educated myself in school and life. My parents have been a huge inspiration to me, they both were immigrants, and despite having limited education and no English skills, my dad became a successful business owner that supported a family of nine.

N. No is not an option- In my personal life and business, I have heard a lot of no's. Do not take it personally. All Of those no's have gotten me closer to the yeses.

O. Opportunities- I have learned to convert challenges into growth opportunities. I ask myself what can I learn from this experience? What is the next step for me to take? Who do I have to be to achieve the result I want?

Conclusion

My dream has always been to educate and inspire others to realize their full potential, see themselves as the great contribution that they are to their families, communities, and life. My purpose is to be the catalyst that propels women to create, develop and bring awareness to their own beauty and self-worth. My goal is that my story will empower women to continue to grow through education, develop leadership skills, exercise the power of leverage, and build their strength through resources and opportunities.

EYES WIDE SHUT TO DEFYING THE ODDS

Tonya Kent

Why Me?

How did I go through Elementary, Junior High, and High School without someone noticing that I was dyslexic? During my era of growing up, instead of educators getting to my root issue, they decided what was best for me, and often this included passing me along with my grades fluctuating from Bs to Ds.

If you can remember, during the '60s, Ds were considered a passing grade. By the grace of God, I managed to graduate from Berkeley High School with a GPA of 3.0. And so, I believe that it's crucial for me to tell my story. Me sharing my story is called paying it forward.

Being diagnosed with Dyslexia does not define who you are. Many people who have Dyslexia have not developed ways to improve their reading, writing, and speaking skills. I am here to help those who feel defeated because of this disorder. I want to reach people all over the world that I may never see in person who can relate to my story through the reading of this book. Come with me on this journey as I discuss how I discovered the beauty of being Dyslexic and that it doesn't define who I am.

You're Not the Only One

Dyslexia is a learning disorder that affects your ability to read, spell, write, and speak. Kids who have it are often smart and hardworking, but they have trouble connecting the letters they see to the sounds those letters make. About 5% to 10% of Americans have some symptoms of dyslexia, such as slow reading, trouble spelling, or mixing up words.

Dyslexic to Degrees

My name is Tonya Kent. I am a mother, a grandmother, a sister, and a friend. I was born in Berkeley, California, where I was raised by my grandmother. Growing up was not a pretty picture for me. More often than I can remember, I was told by adults, *"Do as I say and not as I do."* I lived in a home where verbal and physical abuse were both frequent and extremely violent, which eventually led to the premature death of both my grandmother and mother.

Like a shadow, the same abuse followed me from childhood into my adult life. At the age of thirty-one, I was married with three children and in an abusive relationship. The pain was so severe and overwhelming, that I often heard voices telling me I should die, that I was not worth living, and my husband did not love me.

During these times, the thoughts began to consume me, and as a result, I became emotional. As I continued listening to the lies from the voices in my head, the words eventually took root, causing me to take pills in an attempt to commit suicide. I felt that life had gotten the best of me. I thought taking the pills would end my life; however, God spared me, and I was given a second chance.

One year after my suicide attempt, I realized my grandmother and mother had lived through this same type of emotional abuse. I left the abusive marriage, and at the age of thirty-four, I enrolled in Solano Community College. It was during this time that it was discovered that I could not read or write beyond an eighth-grade level. I was later diagnosed with Dyslexia. I was told that Dyslexia impacted my ability to read, write, and ultimately my ability to speak clearly. Upon hearing this news, old memories from my years in high school began to resurface. I could recall hearing my biology teacher call me dumb and stupid because I could not comprehend the terminology.

I continued to pursue my goal, which was to complete college and get a degree so that I could have a job with a good-paying salary as a single mother of four kids. As I applied myself, many teachers took interest in investing their time and resources in me to achieve my degrees. What would take an average person of two years to complete a degree took me a total of 10 years with a four-year gap.

By the time I completed SCC, I had received three degrees and one certificate. Being at SCC opened many doors of opportunity, such as going on a seventeen-day Civil Rights Tour with my literacy sponsor. On the tour, we visited Martin Luther King Jr.'s hometown, Mississippi, and Tennessee. We also met alive and well activists that were a part of the Civil Rights Movement.

Visiting the different sites encouraged me to get a higher education. After all, it was my ancestors' who fought for my education. I worked hard to achieve a GPA that would transfer me to the University of California Davis (UC Davis) in the Fall of 2015. In addition, I was accepted as an inaugural member of the Community College Pathways to Law School Initiative Program, where I continued to thrive academically under the mentorship and tutelage of one of my professors.

While attending a political science course at Solano Community College, I became inspired to pursue a career in law. This course helped me to understand the perils my three younger brothers, as well as countless other individuals, face as they endure the hardships of trials and the daunting battle of not receiving proper legal representation.

Now, I thought learning was hard at the Community College level, and boy was I in over my head when I started UC Davis. In my first year at UC Davis, I had heavy reading requirements and weekly writing assignments. During this time, my brain was stretched to a capacity I did not believe was possible. There were many times throughout the first two years at UC Davis, I would walk from the campus to my apartment and cry out to God. I would find myself comparing myself to others, asking Him why couldn't I be like this person or that person? His answer was,

"Before I formed you in the womb, I knew you, and before you were born, I consecrated you; I appointed you to be a prophet to the nations."

(Jeremiah 1:5)

I praised Him for lifting my spirits to continue even though it was difficult. As I followed the advice of my professors, I experienced the fruit of being able to read, write, and comprehend the class materials. I began reading and writing at the university level. I had favor over my life.

While at UC Davis, I was afforded the opportunity to visit Ghana in Africa for 30 days and completed a 10-week internship in London, UK. I completed UC Davis in the summer of 2017 with a BA degree in African-American Studies. I thought, well I have accomplished a lot but there was more in my belly to achieve. Working with people who suffer from injustice is another passion of mine.

In the Fall of 2017, I got accepted into John F. Kennedy Law School, which I struggled with during the first year. But I did not let that stop me. In the following year, I decided to start the Paralegal Studies Program. This was the best thing I did to help me grasp the material that I learned in law school. In the Fall of 2019, I completed law school with a Paralegal Certificate.

I was able to overcome my learning obstacles by making the choice to not give up despite the challenges that I endured. I also learned how to ask for help. I followed the advice of my college professors, who said, *"The more you read the better your reading skills will become."* I was also told that writing is a lifelong process, and over time my writing skills would improve.

Despite all the challenges that might make another person give up, I fought hard to defeat the odds against me and achieve more degrees and certificates than I could imagine.

Overcoming the Lies that Plague my Mind

Although I was diagnosed with being Dyslexic, I overcame the challenges that come with this disorder and this is where I am today. Today, I can read, write, and spell. Today, I have a voice to tell the world how I overcame the struggles with being Dyslexic. This was my approach toward the plagues I was faced with for over 20 years.

1. I had to accept that I was Dyslexic. I was not dumb, but I learned differently than others.

2. I had to change my mindset. I couldn't believe the lie, that if you have dyslexia, you are dumb and stupid. Yes, I struggled with connecting the dots in reading comprehension, but I wasn't retarded.

3. I had to recognize there was help for me, but I needed to ask for it. There were sponsors that wanted to invest in my education; I had to put shame down and pick up trust.

4. I had to realize it was okay that I learned differently from others. It was okay that I had to read paragraphs multiple times to understand the material.

5. I had to look up unfamiliar words and grasp the meaning over and over again. At the beginning of my journey of learning how to read, write, and spell, it took me a long time to get through one paragraph because I wasn't familiar with the words I was reading. I started a list of words and wrote out the definition because I knew I would see the words over and over again. This was a way for me to get that word in my memory bank.

6. I had to expand my reading with different genres. I read the Bible, magazines, the newspaper, textbook literature, and books about other people who had overcome the lies about being Dyslexic.

7. I had to retrain my brain to do something different, which was to continue reading and writing as often as I could. Now, it makes sense as to why the devil wanted me to stay poor and illiterate because he recognized the power that God has given me to spread the good news to others. We don't have to keep the cards that were dealt to us. We have the power to change our story.

8. Lastly, I constantly remind myself, I will not give up no matter what. I had to be my own cheerleader from time to time. Giving up wasn't an option for me. Had I given up, I wouldn't be here sharing my story today. The struggles were real, but it was all worth it. Reading, writing, and spelling has given me the opportunity to be a blessing to my children, grandchildren, family, friends, and others I may not ever meet by sharing my story of Dyslexic to Degrees.

Never Give Up

Despite all the challenges that might make another person give up, I fought hard to develop literacy and worked with many sponsors at Solano Community College, an undergrad student at the University of California Davis, as well as a law student at John F. Kennedy Law School, and Jezreel School of Theology. Once I realized I had the help I needed, it was up to me to use the resources available to me in order to excel in my education. I lined myself up with literacy sponsors and the fruit from the different relationships with my academic instructors, which helped me start excelling in literacy.

Giving up was never an option for me, but applying my tools was one of the best decisions I ever made for myself. I encourage all who struggle with being dyslexic to not let it define who you are, but to apply yourself and connect with the different tools and support that you can utilize to help you overcome the challenges. I am one resource that will be willing to support you to the best of my ability, along with prayer.

Adults can have this learning disorder as well. Some people are diagnosed early in life. Others don't realize they have dyslexia until they get older. (WebMD Medical Reference Reviewed by Dan Brennan, MD on March 23, 2019)

According to Dyslexia Facts and Statistics, October is Dyslexia Awareness Month. To raise awareness and dispel misconceptions about Dyslexia, I have compiled a list of facts and statistics about Dyslexia.

» It is estimated that 1 in 10 people have dyslexia

» Over 40 million American adults are dyslexic – and only 2 million know it

» 80% of people associate dyslexia with some form of retardation - this is not true

» Dyslexics may struggle with organizational skills, planning and prioritizing, keeping time, and concentrating with background noise

» Dyslexics may excel at connecting ideas, thinking out of the box, 3D thinking, and seeing the big picture

» People with dyslexia excel or are even gifted in areas of art, computer science, design, drama, electronics, math, mechanics, music, physics, sales, and sports

» Dyslexia occurs in people of all backgrounds and intellectual levels

» Dyslexia runs in families; parents with dyslexia are likely to have children with dyslexia

EXAMPLES: Many famous people have dyslexia, including, Orlando Bloom, Whoopi Goldberg, Stephen Spielberg, and Albert Einstein, According to Austin Learning Solutions.

SOURCES: *American Dyslexia Association, The International Dyslexia Association, The Dyslexia Center, The Dyslexia Foundation, The Child Mind Institute* (Solutions, n.d.)

LIVING FOR MYSELF

Tammy Lyons

Some of us grow up believing in the Cinderella fairytale, that our knight in shining armor would come and save us. But the truth is there is no knight in shining armor. There are no fairy tales except what we make for ourselves. If I kept believing that if I did all the things I was raised to believe, then my prince would come. And if I did all that he wanted, he would bring me happiness. My happiness was based on following the rules. It is so archaic to think in those terms in today's society. But believe me we did.

It took me a long time to realize that if I wanted to do something I had to do it for myself and not for others, especially not a man. As a woman, it took me a long time to realize that I did not need a man in my life to be whole. I could do it on my own, under my rules. In my many relationships, and I mean many, I always tried to please the other person, but I was missing something. I was not feeding my own needs, wants, and desires. It was not until years later that I realized I was codependent. It was my mistaken belief that I was just being empathic. It was a way to show I loved the person I was with by being all consumed by them.

If they wanted something I was going to get it for them. If they desired something, I would go out of my way to obtain it for them. This unhealthy way of life was slowly destroying the person I was meant to be. It is virtually impossible to live for someone else and not feel resentment, depression, or a total lack of self-worth. My self-esteem was at an all-time low. I knew that I had to do something. I was slowly destroying myself from the inside out.

I put aside my own feelings, wants, and desires to be 100% available for someone else. I was literally living the life of waiting by the phone for it to ring. I was unable to speak for myself. What did I want in life? Where did I want to go? I was always afraid to answer the question in fear my answer would be rebuffed. I never spoke up as I feared rejection. In my mind, it was easier to give in and suppress my own feelings than being rejected. I would swallow myself whole and do anything I could, to please the person I was with even at my own detriment.

All I would answer to any question was, "Whatever you want." This was not the way to live a fulfilling life. I knew at some point I would crack. In order to change myself, I had to learn what my issue was in life. Why did I surrender myself to someone else? I knew that it was not a healthy way to deal with issues. The life best lived is the life we live for ourselves. I was unhappy and unfulfilled. I needed to "own it." Own my own emotions.

Searching for the Truth

Why did I put others first? I researched my issues and found that the answer was simple, I was codependent. More than 90% of Americans display some type of codependent behavior during their lifetime. Codependency is defined by an unhealthy or obsessive dependence on another person. One's own identity cannot be contingent upon someone else. Codependency does not allow a relationship to grow and flourish. It can quickly burn out and die as embers left in a fireplace.

Although studies show that people in codependent relationships suffer from drug abuse or alcoholism that is not always the case. Some individuals develop unhealthy codependent relationships due to unstable childhoods. If a child takes on more responsibility when young, then they can develop unhealthy relationships when they grow into adulthood. They feel responsible for anything and everything that happens.

Characteristics of codependent individuals demonstrate low self-esteem, obsessiveness, people-pleasing behaviors and have difficulty setting boundaries. The most common stereotype is that women suffer from codependency more than men. This assumption is false as there is no evidence to point to that. Research has pointed to personality traits over gender. Given that I am a woman, does not make me more susceptible to being codependent than my male counterpart.

Who am I?

I was born in Corona, California to a young unwed mother. For the first few years of my life, I was raised by my grandparents. They loved me unconditionally. It was not until I was older that I learned my grandparents were going to adopt me, but my mother met my stepfather and he insisted on raising me. He was the best father a daughter could ever want. I never knew the truth until I was in my teens. My mother treated me differently, but my father treated us all alike. I had two younger sisters. He loved to take the three of us to baseball games. Not just any team but the Angels. We all grew up loving that baseball team.

My life was not easy. What you saw on the outside did not match the truth of the situation. I could feel the tension in the house. My mother was not easy to get along with and she did not work, and my father provided for us all. Perhaps that is where the prince charming syndrome came into play. Be the doting wife and mother even though the truth was a different story.

Why Me?

Growing up, I was always afraid to voice my opinion. It was better to be silent than to be noticed. In silence, you are thrown to the side. You will not be sought out. I remember the loud voices around me. The arguments from spending money to working late. I often hid in my closet reading. Reading was my escape from the voices that surrounded me. Reading allowed me to transform to another place. To visit places, I never imagined I would ever see in real life. I could be anyone I wanted to be. I could experience sights and sounds that I only dreamed about in my sleep. At one point I wanted to be *Nancy Drew* as I turned the pages of her latest sleuth novel.

Reading opened a whole new world to me, and I knew that if I wanted those things, I read about I needed an education. I did not come from educated stock. In my family, there was always an excuse as to why someone did not pursue those dreams. There was always a reason why nothing was ever good enough. I was not good enough. So, I threw myself into my studies. A true book geek. Geeks nowadays are rock stars but not back then, they were more someone to be shunned. In my world, I believed I needed straight "As" to make it into college. I thought college was an impossible goal as no one in my immediate family graduated from college. You were lucky if you graduated from high school.

In the movies, it was always the prettiest, smartest, and the wealthiest that went to college, all of the things I believed I was not. I had no one to look up to or ask how I got to B from point A. I was terrified of school counselors as I was already labeled a problem child in my family. To this day, I have no idea why because I was the only one bringing home the grades and ambition to continue on.

Looking back, I can see my codependent tendencies even back in high school. I wanted to be liked. I wanted to be loved. I would do anything for anyone, from doing my friends' homework to agreeing to anything no matter the consequences. Codependency can materialize at any age at any time.

When the Bough Breaks, Fix it.

Unfortunately, because of this personality trait, I took the long road towards my dreams. My codependency led me to a horrible early marriage and a pregnancy, however, I did not let that stop me. Eventually, I saw the light. All I wanted to do was please the person I was with and going to college was not pleasing in his eyes. Perhaps he felt it would have elevated me out of the situation I was in and that was something that my partner did not want. I was by all accounts the dutiful wife and mother, but I was sinking in my own self-worth. There was no money, and I was not allowed to work. I needed to be at his beck and call every minute. I knew I could not continue living that way. I felt I was in the endless cycle that I swore I would break when I was young. I always wanted to go to college and be somebody.

Even through my time sitting in my closet reading I truly believed I was meant for something more than merely existing. I felt like I was trapped in the 1950s and I was more of a free spirit than a 50's stay-at-home uneducated woman. Funny how stereotypes affect our personality and our ambitions. I saw the way my mother acted, not really her own person but blaming everyone for her predicament.

At times, she would say she wanted more, but she never tried for more than what she had at that point. She never reached for the stars. She put blame on having children as to why she was the way she was, and I did not want that for me. I wanted to show my girls that because you are a woman, it does not have to keep you down. You do not have to be all behooving to a man. You can reach for the stars and not rely on a man to put food on the table. Your partner does not define you. You define you.

So, I hit my breaking point, crying every night on the floor of the bathroom. Not wanting to live the life I was given. I once again wanted more. I wanted to bring home the bacon and fry it in the pan. I wanted to buy some new clothes. I wanted to pull out the cash and say, "I will take it." Not ask for permission. It was my money, and I would do what I wanted with it. If I wanted something, then I was going to get it. I'd be damned if I had to ask anyone anymore for permission.

Moving Forward

How do you move from A to B? Sometimes you cannot do it alone, you need help. You need to believe in yourself and surround yourself with positive people who will lift you up and surround you with love.

1. I read a lot of books on codependency. Searched the internet for anything that referenced co-dependent behaviors.

2. I cut out all the negative people from my life. If they could not say anything positive, then they were gone. If they were not supporting the "new" me, then I did not need them in my life.

3. I had the courage to pursue my dreams.

4. I filled my life with "yes" women. They lifted me up when I needed it the most.

5. I enrolled in graduate school.

6. I meditated.

7. Most importantly I was not afraid to fail. – *"Failure is not the absence of trying. The absence of trying is a failure."* My mantra.

It has not been easy. I remember times when I cried in the shower because I did not think I would make it through. I had to give myself up to believe in myself. Not being afraid to dream once again. It took longer than expected but I did graduate from law school. I was able to practice law and show my girls that they can do it. I was able to do it on my own. My dream of a knight in shining armor may not have come true but my dream of being my own person was fulfilled.

H.E.R. A.C.T.

Dr. Merary Simeon

Betrayal, doubt, depression, fear, and pain, I know you too well. I have battled on the front-lines of societal pressures and transformed into the woman I am today. Past experiences, trauma, cultural messaging, and hurtful words can make your heart their home and your mind, a playground for doubt. While I have thrived in the face of adversity, limiting beliefs held me back from achieving my fullest potential. For a long time, the limiting beliefs I carried held me captive from enjoying the fruit of the Spirit.

"The fruit of the Spirit is love, joy, peace, longsuffering, kindness, goodness, faithfulness, gentleness, and self-control." (Galatians 5:22-23)

Everyone has the right to delight in the fruit of the Spirit and own their narrative. I'm on a journey to share my learnings and empower every woman to activate her transformation and realize her power through the H.E.R. A.C.T. framework. The H.E.R. A.C.T. framework highlights the importance of **H**ealing, **E**levating your mindset, and learning to **R**espect and love yourself to **A**chieve **C**onfidence and **T**ransformation. There is urgency; the world needs the talents you possess, it is time for self-revolution. It is time to arise and shine!

Uninvited Guests

I believe every woman has powerful and unique gifts planted in her specifically to achieve her Divine purpose. Yet, the uninvited guests I like to call limiting beliefs, are ready and able to destroy us if we allow them. Limiting beliefs are inaccurate thoughts about ourselves. Studies confirm limiting beliefs negatively influence workplace performance and prevent your career advancement, (Dickerson & Taylor, 2000). They restrain us from taking risks and maximizing our potential as a businesswoman, wife, mother, sister, and a friend. Limiting beliefs feed and strengthen fear, greed, rage, resentment, shame, blame, and indifference. It does not only negatively impact our ability to succeed in the marketplace; it makes our everyday, hell.

Leaders genuinely struggling with identifying and accepting a past left undealt with will cripple their long-term success, (Blackaby & Blackaby, 2011). Sadly, many people experiencing limiting beliefs miss out on the joys of life, waiting for others' approval. Instead, bitterness moves in and cripples them while they secretly resent those who succeed.

People who experience limiting beliefs avoid stepping out of their comfort zone, making it impossible to transform. The same way a butterfly must leave behind her old self to achieve its beauty and authentic self, a woman must step out of her comfort zone to realize her purpose.

The McKinsey & Company Centered of Leadership Research found the increase of women in the workplace is a factor in the United States economy's success. The same research also cited limiting beliefs are a barrier to a woman's success, (Barsh & Yee, 2011). Limiting thoughts are destructive and deserve our attention because when a woman overcomes limiting beliefs, she is limitless. Achieving your dreams or living in a nightmare is determined by how we respond to life's positive and undesirable experiences. Our daily decisions move us closer or further from our personal-transformation and our truth. Today, I choose to live in the truth, and so can you.

Peace is Priceless

I was born in Puerto Rico. Puerto Rico is known for its enchantment of beauty everywhere you look. Even the poor have majestic views. We did not have much, but we had enough; we had a home, love, food on the table, and the freedom to smell the fresh air, laugh, play, and enjoy the beauty of the island every day. In the search for the American dream, our parents moved to a small town in New Jersey.

I still remember being both fearful and excited about the new adventure of moving to the United States. Life was about to change for all of us and not for the best. We went from living in the beautiful farms of Puerto Rico where you could run free to living in a dreary, dark, and cold basement.

A basement where the sun did not shine, and the cold pierced your bones. I went from sharing a room with my oldest sister to seven of us living in an open space basement with no privacy. Excitement quickly faded away, and resentment began to plant seeds in my heart. Violence and alcohol ruled the surroundings—something I had never experienced until moving to New Jersey.

In time, my parents had enough money to move into a small apartment where we could walk in through a standard door and the sunlight shined through the windows. My parents continued to work two jobs to make ends meet and were never home. We no longer were the family we once were.

Attending school was a nightmare; I went from being a 4.0 student to barely making a passing grade. Not only was learning the language challenging but being in survival mode each day took a toll. I was expelled from three schools because surviving literally meant physical fights to protect myself and those I loved. It was not long before I hooked up with the wrong crowd. At age 14, I drank in school and got high on the weekends to ease the hate, resentment, and anger I carried with me each day. All my siblings quit school, and our home was no longer our haven. As teenagers, the pressures of the environment weighed heavy on some of my friends. We lost friends to suicide or drugs.

Despite my surroundings, I knew I needed to help the family financially. At fifteen, I was working cleaning toilets in an office building. One day, I saw a helicopter land on the office's helipad. Two men in suits walked off the helicopter into their shiny cars. On that day, I decided I would do everything in my power to escape poverty.

I had no mentors, role models, or the slightest idea of achieving success and escaping poverty. Probably the best thing that happened to me was when I took an auto shop class in high school not to pay a mechanic to fix my car. It was only a matter of time before the principal kicked me out of school, and the judge revoked my license until my eighteenth birthday.

In hopes of a transformation, my parents sent me to Puerto Rico. A personal change did not take place, but it did remove me from a toxic environment. I continued to drink and influence others to follow my bad behavior. In my junior year, I was able to return to New Jersey. I was now in a physically abusive relationship. I lost count of the times my friends intervened, and I swore I would never go back. I used to ask God to give me a sign to walk away, and He always did. I chose not to listen. Betrayal now grew in my heart as my abusive boyfriend cheated on me with a friend I loved.

One day while half asleep sitting in class, the principal announces a scholarship opportunity for the student who wrote the best essay. I immediately thought, this is it; I can get into college if I win this contest and change my future. I asked my English teacher what I needed to do to enter the essay contest. She immediately replied, *"Do not waste your time; you are not smart enough, and you are going to end up pregnant and on drugs like all your friends in school."*

I think she saw that the odds were against me; many high school girls were pregnant, dropouts, or on drugs. My hopes chartered until my business teacher, Mrs. Bolden, saw my potential, something I did not see in myself. We agreed if I learned the business class and taught those who needed help in class and got everyone to finish their work on time, she would let the students have a free period. I immediately went to work; I learned and spent one-on-one time with each student. We got it done. We did a potluck; I created certificates of completion and presented them to each student to celebrate our achievements. I asked her if I should write the essay, and she immediately answered, *"Why wouldn't you?"* She gave me confidence; she restored my hope. I wrote the essay, and I won. Imagine if I would have listened to my English teacher. I would not be here today telling you this story.

When I told my parents I won a scholarship, the joy I saw in their eyes gave me life. On that day, I promised myself they would see one of their children graduate high school. Mrs. Bolden became the mentor I needed. She sponsored me for a year-round high school internship with a Fortune 100 company. Despite my track record, she recognized my potential and took a chance on me.

On day one of my training, my new boss told me other students knew my past and advised the hiring manager not to give me the opportunity. She went on to say, the only reason I got the job was that Mrs. Bolden was my sponsor. On that day, I promised myself that I would not let Mrs. Bolden down. I owe my career to Mrs. Bolden; she saw my potential in the middle of chaos. She nurtured my leadership skills, guided me in the right direction, and saved me from myself.

I graduated high school and quickly moved up in the organization. I worked three jobs and attended college at night and on the weekend. Money was no longer an issue, and I was able to help my parents. An anxiety attack forced me to quit one of my part-time jobs. Because I had not dealt with the hate, bitterness, and anger, the free time I now had, led me back to drinking and hanging out with the wrong people.

I was making good money and had nothing to show for it. On my college graduation day, I got so drunk; I never made it to the graduation. My parents and loved ones waited to see me walk, I was the first to graduate college, but I never showed up. I cried. I was filled with shame and anger for days. Fast forward to another toxic relationship. I spent 12 years in a new mental and emotional prison.

My confidence was gone, and my insecurities increased by the day. His disloyalty grew each day, and for years, I believed it was my fault. I attempted to run away from the relationship more times than I can count and failed each time miserably. At one point, I was willing to die to get away from the relationship.

God had bigger plans for me, and by His grace, I escaped another toxic relationship. One day, I woke up-scholarly accomplished and financially stable with a high-profile executive job. My perseverance had paid off. Yet, what should have been a time of happiness, contentment, and purpose, felt more like void, torment, anger, and agony. The trauma, life experiences, and damaging cultural messaging, now ruled over my heart and mind. Success no longer tamed the hurt. The dreams I worked so hard to achieve, I now detested. Depression took center stage. Limiting beliefs haunted me and attempted to stop me from achieving my fullest potential.

I pursued material things, status, physical appearance, titles, acceptance, and a career. Only to later find not one of them brought me peace. Even though I walked away from painful environments, I had not healed from my past. I moved once again in hopes of running away from it all and starting new. Still, the torment accompanied me everywhere I went.

During one of my business trips to Brazil, I remember calling my mother and telling her the thoughts in my head wanted to take my breath away. I could not accept these feelings, and I asked her to pray for me over the phone. I remember feeling at peace. Years passed, and while I continued to gain success, feeling trapped and in desperation, I went to a local church. It was there, my transformation from the inside out began. The day I walked into that church, the Holy Spirit filled me with joy, and I wanted more. There was a lot to unpack in my past and fears I needed to face. The shift did not happen overnight, but each day God opened my eyes to something new.

Each day, there was a choice I needed to make, and my peace depended on my obedience. It was simple, yet so hard. I needed to seek the Kingdom of God and His righteousness as described in Matthew 6:33. It was clear the days I did not seek Him, my transformation would stall, and depression and loneliness would begin to knock on the doors to my heart and mind. To transform, required my full attention and commitment. After realizing I could not change without God, I entered into a relationship with Jesus. Through Him, I resisted temptation and found the strength to overcome the limiting beliefs holding me back from achieving the fruit of the Spirit.

ACTivate H.E.R. A.C.T.

Based on life experiences and supported by research, I discovered H.E.R. A.C.T., a sustainable self-transformation method. H.E.R. A.C.T. is practical, yet it will empower you to own your narrative. Our life experiences will not always be pleasant ones. We will encounter people and situations that bring us pain. H.E.R. A.C.T. prepares you to face problems, address them, and move forward with self-confidence and peace. You too, can experience freedom, delight in the fruit of the Spirit, and own your narrative.

H-Healing is the foundation of transformation. It begins with forgiveness. Through the power of healing, you can step into your self-transformational journey.

"He heals the brokenhearted and binds up their wounds." Psalm 147:3

E-Elevate your mindset to ACTivate a life filled with a divine purpose.

"Do not conform to the things of this world, but be transformed by the renewing of your mind." Romans 12:2

R- Respect and love yourself the way God made you.

"I am fearfully and wonderfully made." Psalm 139:14

A-Achieve your dreams by leveraging your strengths.

"I can do all things through Christ who strengthens me." Philippians 4:13

C-Confidence is within you, do not discard it. Persevere and live in your purpose.

"And my God will supply every need of yours." Philippians 4:19

T-Transformation from the inside out is achievable. It is time to shine.

"You are the light of the word, a city set on a hill cannot be hidden."
– Matthew 5:15

Arise & Shine

I hope H.E.R. A.C.T. empowers you woman to activate your gifts and live a life with purpose and spiritual peace. The secret to activating H.E.R. A.C.T. and achieving a sustainable self-transformation, is inviting Jesus Christ into your life. You, too, can delight in the fruits of the Spirit and own your narrative. Your commitment to ACTivating H.E.R. A.C.T. in your life will empower you to re-write your story and experience a sustainable, life-changing transformation. Arise today and choose to ACTivate H.E.R. A.C.T. You are loved. You are worthy. You are worth the fight!

Bibliography

Barsh, J., & Yee, L. (2011). Unlocking the full potential of women in the US economy. McKinsey & Company, (April).

Blackaby, H. T., & Blackaby, R. (2011). Spiritual leadership: Moving People on to God's agenda. B&H Publishing Group.

Dickerson, A., & Taylor, M. A. (2000). Self-limiting behavior in women: Self-esteem and self-efficacy as predictors. Group & Organization Management, 25(2), 191-210. doi:10.1177/1059601100252006

Empowerment To Overcome Difficult Issues

"It's the tough things that we go through, hard things we go through, that get us to that point where we're better and stronger than we've ever been."-DMX

Self-Doubt to Empowered Success

Dr. Margarita David DNP, RN, PCCN, CSN

Although my official name is Dr. David, I have always been known as Eliza to my family and friends. Why do I mention this? Because the way I have been known, portrayed, and imagined were consistently two distinct forces on the professional and personal level. To go through an internal and emotional turmoil of not belonging and feeling excluded, but at the same time doing things that will, at least in my mind, allow me the opportunity to belong, can be detrimental.

This constant battle between my struggles, aspirations, and feelings of wanting to belong played a key role in overcoming obstacles in my younger years, my development, and who I am today; one full of flaws like you.

Did you think you were alone on this journey called life? Guess what? You are not. As successful as I am, I have gone through both internal and external struggles. These struggles served as the gasoline to light up a future full of empathy, gratitude, and an overall feeling of empowerment. This empowerment leads to the ability to empower others to not view themselves as perfect, but as the sum of many experiences, negative or positive. The culmination of experiences serves as the energy source that has helped me to accept my flaws and help me succeed. Come join me on this transformation from self-doubt and lack of self-acceptance, to embracing my flaws for a purposeful, and empowering transformation.

The Person-Defined

Self-acceptance means to completely accept ourselves and embrace all parts of ourselves including the negative or limiting parts. When we are self-accepting, we are able to unconditionally recognize, and accept our weaknesses, in order to fully embrace who we are. The problem is that we need to learn these self-accepting behaviors by a certain age, or we will have a hard time believing in our capabilities.

Surprisingly, research has shown that before a child is eight years old, the ability to formulate a clear sense of who they are, is determined by those that care for us. Why is this an important concept to understand? Because as children, we gather a sense of self, based on how those around us, specifically our parents, nurture and accept us. If our caretakers were unable to communicate messages of acceptance, then we would have a sense of not belonging, and an overall feeling of inadequacy. Additionally, studies have shown that children who struggle with self-acceptance due to feeling inadequate, are more likely to grow up to be depressed, isolated, and lack the ability to show affection. Knowing this now makes me reflect on my childhood, and analyze the roller coaster of feelings I had, and continue to have today.

Although I had a great childhood with the support of my mother and grandparents, there was someone missing, my biological dad. Even though my grandfather served as a father figure, and my mother married a man that to this day I call "dad," and later remarried the father of my two sisters, I always felt a sense of loss. I always wondered as to why I saw other children with both of their parents, and why it had to be me that walked around with my mom and grandparents by my side?

To continuously wonder about what half of my DNA looked like, was always lingering in my thoughts. To know that about 70% of children that grow up without a biological father struggle academically, personally, and professionally as their self-esteem can be irreparably damaged, made a lot of sense as to how I felt, and I was scared to become the next statistic.

The Hurt

These feelings became more and more intense as I grew older and realized that the absence of a biological father was starting to have a negative impact on my self-esteem. I know you will say, "But her grandfather served as the father figure," and although you are right, I still felt a void. A void that many didn't understand, not even me. A void that became more pronounced in my internal and emotional turmoil with the arrival of my sisters. A void that was to blame for my rebellious behavior, which earned me the title of the family's "black sheep."

A void that became a bleeding wound when the feeling of exclusion took over me, as I didn't feel part of the "family circle" that I was "part of." A void that has played a major role in my lack of showing affection towards everyone around me, including my children, and alienating myself from others. A void, that every now and then, makes me hide in a room, and cry tears of a multitude of feelings, especially when I reflect on how much I have accomplished even when faced with adversities and obstacles. A void that to this day remains open, but that I have managed to use throughout the years, as an energy source to do better, even when I didn't want to. A void that you won't see, but that I feel every day.

Through all these struggles, I was also expected to succeed. That expectation and my need to make everyone happy, so that I can somehow be accepted, was driving me crazy. Imagine going through these issues, while maintaining excellent grades because anything less was not acceptable? Additionally, when it came to my sisters and I, there was an expectation of me, and then a totally different one for them. How is that possible you may ask? Simple. I was my mother's daughter and my sisters had both parents. Well, at least that was the response I always received. What does this mean?

Their father was more liberal than my mom, therefore they tended to have more freedoms while my freedoms consisted of home and school. This continues in different ways to this day. Can you see why as I grew older, I continued to struggle with feeling like I didn't belong? I was continuously reminded that there were two sets of rules, and I always got the short end of the stick. However, this was not my mother's fault, as she was responsible for me and wanted the best, however to this day she doesn't understand how I perceived things. I wondered, why not treat all of us the same? Why not provide the same freedoms and punishments?

As a result, I always felt not wanted as I was not my stepfather's child, and to this day my sisters are still treated differently than me. In no way do I want to blame my mom, but her compliance with the behaviors was to my detriment. I consider my mom my best friend, and we talk multiple times a day. At times, I tend to dwell on the past and remind her and my sisters of my feelings, and often say to them, "Don't worry, it doesn't bother me anymore," even when it still does.

Do you think it doesn't bother me to see that my sisters as adults, now with children of their own, are celebrated with balloons and cake on their birthdays? Do you think it doesn't bother me that when something is happening, I am, on most occasions, excluded from conversations because "I am dramatic?" Of course, it does, but I have learned to compartmentalize my feelings, and this is the defense mechanism that I have created so that I don't explode.

These feelings are the reason that for each of my children, I had a different parenting style. My oldest received the brunt of my negative side. As we grow up, we always say that when we are parents, we will do things differently for our children. Although I held the same belief, I struggled when raising my firstborn. I used the same pressures on him, without even noticing. It was like repeating the "you need to be successful or else" cycle. This had a negative impact on him, causing him to be isolating and distant, and for this, I will forever feel a sense of failure. However, as the seasons change, so do people and when it comes to my son and my other children, things are looking positive.

Now, you may say but you have achieved so much in life, and are successful, so why worry about all that stuff? It came a time when I decided to stop answering that specific question. The better question should be, "Is your overachieving behavior a defense mechanism created in order to prove that you are worthy and accepted?" And to this question, I answer YES. I am what is called an "insecure overachiever."

An insecure overachiever is not born this way but made this way, due to experiencing some form of psychological or physical insecurity. When I found this definition, everything made sense. However, I knew that I had to change this perception of myself because I enjoyed being successful but wanted to make sure it was for the right reasons. At that point is when I decided to change my internal algorithm.

The Healing

The first step in reinventing myself internally and externally was to become aware of what my own motivations were and identify what success meant for me. I knew that my transformation would not be easy, and it is a work in progress, but all I could do was try. I had come to the realization that if I were to overcome some of my earlier internal struggles, I had to do my part. With this realization, I decided to practice the following steps that helped me to be mindful of my surroundings, acknowledge my feelings, and accept my flaws in order for me to be successful in all aspects of my life:

1. Acknowledge that not everything can be right all the time and give myself the proper amount of time to explore my thought process and prevent negative thoughts.

2. Be kind to myself by practicing self-compassion, which helps me accept my mistakes and value my strengths.

3. Focused on my strengths while understanding my weaknesses while reaching realistic goals.

4. Be accepting of others as I cannot control how they behave, think, or feel.

5. Accept that some things in life cannot be changed because I cannot control how others behave, think, or feel and that it is normal as humans to experience pain, frustration, and anger.

6. Accept what is happening right now, stop dwelling on the past, and what may happen in the future, which can cause both stress and anxiety.

Once I started practicing these steps, I was able to help myself think and feel better. Don't get me wrong, this is a process that takes time and constant practice, but it has allowed me to look at my thoughts and feelings differently. It has allowed me to give myself room for mistakes, and to accept my flaws as best as I can without being hard on myself. Above all, it has allowed me to look at my situation and those around me and be accepting of who they are, so that I am able to move forward.

In Closing

Going through a roller coaster ride full of emotional turns and struggles, to reaching a point in my life where I have accepted what transpired and how my flaws played a role in the process, has allowed me the opportunity to accept every part of me. I know now that me being who I am or how others made me feel, is not the issue. Accepting who I was, am, and am becoming, is the strength I need to empower my mind and soul to accept my flaws, and purposely move on.

Not everyone's transformation will be the same, but I hope that if you have gone through or are going through a similar experience to mine, that you understand you are not alone. However, know that until you come to terms with what has happened to you, it will be hard to move on and focus on what matters yourself.

Bibliography

Adamsons, K., & Johnson, S. K. (2013). An updated and expanded meta-analysis of nonresident

fathering and child well-being. *Journal of Family Psychology*, 27, 589-599.

Segran, E. (2016). How overachieving parents can avoid ruining their kid's lives. Retrieved from

https://www.fastcompany.com/3059800/how-overachieving-parents-can-avoid-pressuring-their-kids

Whitney, S., Prewett, S., Wang, Ze, & Haigin C. (2017). Fathers' importance in adolescents'

academic achievement. International Journal of Child, Youth and Family Studies, 8(3–4), 101–126.

A Mother's Love

Blanca Solorzano

Yௌou are truly never ready for what life has in store, but when a miracle happens, everything changes. Life becomes a sweet melody. You appreciate every movement with every breath you take because a new life is growing inside of you. The fact is no one can ever prepare you for motherhood. There are no guides or manuals. A mother's love is unlike any other.

My journey as a mother started with challenges and struggles. Some have been easier than others, but nothing is tougher than grieving for a child. Often asking myself why I feel so alone, questioning God every second of each day that passes. I am so angry. Why God? Why my son? I grieve a child that is still on this earth. I made a promise to always protect my son, my miracle. I am struggling to understand what God's plan is for his life. His pain is in my heart and it is broken in pieces. Life will never be the same, my eyes now closing listening to a song he once wrote, I ask the universe, as the beat plays and fades into the distance, to please bring my son back to me.

The toughest battle has now set sail with no answers in place, my struggles and turmoil became so much more real. Can a mother's love save a son's life? These winds are destroying my soul. My child is no longer, he is a stranger, and my faith is diminishing. My wishes to rewind the hands of time are a fantasy. My eyes struggle to remain closed as I yearn to not wake up into this nightmare. As my world crumbles, these winds pierce through my soul and remind me that I must rise from this abyss with strength and resilience. Life has no redoes because the beat keeps playing even when the tape pops.

The Making of Bee

The year was 1982, my sister and I arrived at JFK Airport and we had no idea what life had in store for us. Life was so simple back then, when breakdancing and Cookie Monster on Sesame Street were my favorite things to watch. I was one month shy of my 5th birthday when I arrived in New York. My mother brought us to live in Freeport, NY from El Salvador. I lived and grew up in Freeport, until the age of 18, when I decided to go away to school and move to Boston, Massachusetts.

In the summer of 1996, I enrolled in Boston University and began my journey as an adult and a student. Nonetheless, anything that is super planned never goes as planned. I left Boston and ended up at SUNY StonyBrook University. Getting an education was always a big integral part of my life because I wanted to always set an example. I wanted to be the first one in my family to go to school and become someone despite our struggles and where we came from. Once again, I found myself facing life going down a different path and changing my route.

The Miracle Child

In 1999, I met a young man who I fell in love with. Nothing else in life mattered when I met him. We were inseparable. You always hear people say you know "the one" when you meet them. I never thought I would say it but that is exactly how it was when our eyes met. I saw no other and the world stopped for a split second. I knew then that we would be together forever, and the feeling was mutual. After three years of love and friendship, our son was born.

From the moment I knew I was pregnant with him; I knew he was going to be so special. I nurtured and fed him knowledge from the time he could hear sounds in my womb. He amazed me even then and I loved him unconditionally without even knowing who he was. My son was born in 2002 via c-section.

While growing up, he was always a funny, inquisitive, and a quirky kid. He would often engage in better conversations with adults than with kids his age because he was so eloquent. He loved books and read so much; he would often enter reading contests to win prizes. What a proud mom moment that was every single time. From his love of reading, my son started writing poetry in the form of rhymes and songs. By the age of 9, he was writing full songs and performing them at different venues. My wonderful son was turning into an artist.

His rhyming skills and the way he could remember a beat was amazing at such a young age. He was so full of goals and his love for music seemed to be surpassing all of his previous dreams of playing sports. His father and I nurtured his love and decided to pay for him to have private drumming lessons. We paid for professional studio sessions to record his songs. He was getting so good at his craft, that he was entering competitions and winning awards. Our son was on his way to being a star.

Life Took a Turn

When entering middle school, things started to shift, and we started to notice something physically was not quite the same. Although our son was a good student, we knew something he was going through was stopping him from being himself. We decided to take him to a specialist and found out he was suffering from a tic disorder, which caused movements in his body that he often could not control. We had so many questions and went to so many appointments, but no Dr. could explain what was happening to him.

Tic Disorders fall under the spectrum of Tourette's Syndrome. Studies have shown that there are more than 200,000 cases every year. The effects of this condition are long-lasting. They can be treated, but not cured. This disorder comes with so much more than tics or body movements, it also goes hand-in-hand with hyperactivity, mood disorders ranging from anxiety and insomnia to depression and aggression.

Signs of Tourette's Syndrome usually occur in children ages 7 to 10 but can show up as early as age 2 or as late as age 18. Nonetheless, there is no real underlying cause, and little is known about it, so there is no way of knowing if it is hereditary. Of course, some cases are more severe than others, but again there are always other underlying causes that may determine the severity of the condition.

A lot of people do not know of, or understand this condition, therefore making the person with the condition feel alienated or seem as if they are a nuisance. Hollywood has even made this to be something to be made fun of by making people with this disorder seem crazy and obscene. But in reality, it is a heartbreaking situation. Our son has suffered through severe migraines, body aches, and fatigue from trying to hold back the tics. This disorder has caused him to feel even more socially awkward in an environment that did not accept him to begin with for being outspoken and intelligent. Children and adults are cruel, and our son began to suffer deeply from these circumstances.

From the ages of 11 through 16, our son battled with this physical condition to a point where we thought it would never leave him. His father and I did not know or understand what our son was going through. We were not prepared for the roller coaster ride we were about to take our entire family on. I have prayed so much and read as much trying to find any solution on my own. We did everything possible to keep him from feeling any different from any other kid.

The Battle Continues

By the time our son hit 11th grade, he felt tired, tired of life, tired of everything around him not going as planned. He wanted to be like everyone else and not deal with this disorder. That is when in a matter of six months I saw my son, the joyful, fun, loving, outgoing, intelligent boy go into a deep depression. My son was no longer there. This was someone I did not know. The person we knew had completely shut down and gave up on everything that was real. He lost all interest in school, music, and sports. He no longer had any friends and the ones he did have, never even looked back to ask how he was doing.

He was in a darkness I could not understand, and I felt so hopeless, not being able to help him. I would often ask God why, why him? Why was He allowing my son to suffer so deeply? Why has He allowed my son to succumb to this illness? How did we get to this point? This was not supposed to be like this. My son is so intelligent. How did he go from a bright future to this sunken space? I felt like a mother who buried their child yet tortured by his presence without him being there. One night I even begged God to plague my mind and make me sick instead of allowing our son to be sick. I have never felt so lost and alone, but yet I still prayed every night in the hopes that one day God would give me my son back.

So many sleepless nights. So many battles and arguments with fears of one day coming home to find him gone. We did not know what to expect. Our denial was regressing our son and his cry for help was being ignored. It has been so difficult to grieve for someone who is alive because you see them, and you want to one day close your eyes to wake up and see the person that they were once again. You want to move forward faster than what it takes to heal because they are still alive and there is still hope with every breath that they take.

I have wanted to give up at times and let the wind take me away. I was haunted by my dreams of having my son live a normal life like any other child. It is so confusing to feel so much grief and go through every stage of loss knowing the person you lost is still alive. Yet, through it all, I have remained optimistic and kept pushing. There comes a time in all our lives, that we must be realistic and understand what our true purpose is. God only gives His toughest soldiers the hardest battles to conquer. Therefore, change can only come if you learn to conquer yourself from within.

Love Does Heal

I knew that as hard as my decision would be to help my son, there was only one way. One evening, I took a long walk and as I walked on the path around this lake it became clear to me why I had come here. The road around the lake was crooked, but yet was made to follow as a straight path. It was where Heaven reflected upon the calm ripples of the lake. This was my sanctuary, where peace gave me the strength to find the answers, as I walked this path. I kept walking. Then, something came over me and instead of asking God why, I thanked Him and asked for forgiveness.

Suddenly, I looked down and noticed there were arrows on the ground pointing to the direction of where and without question I needed to follow. I felt so inspired and moved because the signs were all there. I needed to understand that my miracle had not been taken from me. He was still here; he was still my son and I needed to help him get better. I needed to be thankful that he was alive and that his life had not ended, he only needed some rope to help him get out of the hole.

Two months later, I decided as his mother and against his father's wishes, to admit him to the hospital after he suffered a seizure-like episode due to what we now know to be psychosis, which is a mental disorder that impairs thought and emotions. It was one of the hardest decisions I have ever made. It caused so much turmoil between his father and I, but I knew I was doing the right thing. I also understood why his father was so angry with me. Just like myself, he was trying to protect his son and he was afraid for him. I was afraid as well, but I knew he needed to get the help that he deserved.

As parents, it was the longest two and a half weeks of our lives. Everything has its expiration and there has to come a time where you can no longer see the person you love suffering any more. We needed to make sure his brain was ok and that he was not in harm's way because of these seizure-like episodes. During his hospital stay, our son went through diagnostic testing and was given medication. We were so thankful and blessed that his test results came back normal but there was still a lot of psychological turmoil that our son was going through and he requires more help than we expected.

A Conclusion for a New Beginning

Our son has come a long way, but still has so much more to conquer. He has been following his treatment plan and medication. He has made so much progress, he seems to be himself at times. Even though we understand he will always have his good and bad days like everyone else, we feel confident he is on his way to full recovery. Our only goals now are to keep his spirits up and have him enjoy life. I know that the boy I once knew may not be the man I see before my eyes, but I am thankful. I feel blessed to have my son by my side. It is so wonderful to hear my son ask me *"How was your day?"* or hug me and to tell me that he loves me. Things so many people take for granted, that you do not realize you miss until you wish for those words to come back. I do not know

80

what life has in store for my son and I can only hope through our love and faith that he remains inspired to get better and maybe get back to creating so his dreams will come true.

The first steps to helping someone who is suffering from mental health issues are the following:

1. Be open-minded and do not judge the person.

2. Do your research:

3. Stay calm.

4. Do not try and fix the person yourself.

5. Be loving and understanding.

6. Recognize there is a problem.

7. Be compassionate and encouraging.

8. Never lose yourself and stay strong.

9. Do not shy away from seeking professional help.

AND MOST IMPORTANTLY...

10. Never give up on the person who is going through mental distress!

Mental health issues affect us all, no matter the race or gender. People from all walks of life suffer from mental health issues, young and old. Through my experience, I have learned to never give up hope for the person that you love. Know that you are not alone, there are many support groups for families, children, teens, and adults. Always be an advocate and always stay one step ahead of the game.

My transformation in conquering this situation definitely took some trial and error, but I found the following steps gave me clarity:

1. Ask lots of questions about your loved one's symptoms and be persistent with your research. Mental Health is not easy to pinpoint.

2. Do not question why this is happening to you and take yourself out of the equation so you do not ignore the person's cry for help. Say how can I help my loved one and be thankful that you can help.

3. Seek professional help for your loved one. You do not always have the right answers. Also find your own support system, you are not alone.

4. Pray and have faith because God always works in mysterious ways.

5. Lastly, accept the changes and appreciate that your loved one may be going through something, but they are still an amazing person inside;

Once you push forward and forget all the stigmas, you can guarantee a better understanding of the situation. The most important thing is not to turn your back on those that you love who are struggling. Especially, when they do not fully understand what is happening or why this is happening.

Life is not easy and the deeper the scars, the more we are reminded of how we have fought through each storm. Remember that God always has a plan, and everything has its purpose. To my wonderful son, who knew that, that little girl back in 1982 would grow up to be your mom and how you would make a positive difference in this world with your astounding presence, love you always.

THE LAW OF ATTRACTION

Tarsha Howard

"For as he thinks in his heart, so is he." (Proverbs 23:7 NKJV)

Have you ever felt like you attract the same person in a different body? I went through this for most of my adult life, but I could not figure out why. I remember studying about Narcissistic Personality Disorder when I took abnormal psychology during undergrad. Since my major was Criminal Justice, I thought this psychological disorder applied only to criminals. Are you in a relationship where you feel like you are on an emotional rollercoaster and cannot seem to get off?

Well, there is a hidden, dark, sinister, and malevolent force that is lurking in the background to take you out. Unfortunately, in the Black Community, it is not popular to talk about mental illness. However, I feel that it is important to bring awareness to Narcissistic Abuse to heal troubled families in the Black community. If you are a single woman who is dating, then I would like to help you recognize this type of personality before you get deeply involved. If you are a victim of Narcissistic Abuse, the spiritual steps that I outline for the Law of Attraction will help bring healing to your soul. Now, sit back while I tell you about my personal encounter with a Narcissist.

What is Narcissistic Abuse?

Narcissistic abuse is a form of emotional and psychological abuse that affects 158 million people in the United States according to www.psychcentral.com. The one who is the abuser is a Narcissist. According to the Mayo Clinic, Narcissistic Personality Disorder is one of several types of personality disorders and is considered a mental condition. It is an extreme form of selfishness. I believe many women have suffered Narcissistic abuse but are not aware of it, especially in the Black community.

My Story

I grew up in Brooklyn, New York. I had a great childhood. I enjoyed the Summer because we would stay outside until it got dark and often sat on the stoop for hours talking with our friends. Once I graduated from high school, I started going to parties and enjoying life as a young person.

I will never forget the summer of 1993. My best friend at the time asked me to meet her downtown Brooklyn at her job. She worked at a retail store. After we met, a group of guys that she knew, saw us shopping. One of the guys asked her to introduce me. I hesitated, but I decided to talk to him. As we spoke, we found out that we all lived in the same neighborhood in Brooklyn. We took the A train home.

On the way home, he began to tell me about himself. He was six years older than me. I was eighteen and he was twenty-four. I started to sense something was off about him, but I proceeded to give him my phone number.

Once I got home, I did not think anything of the meeting. My friend and I parted ways and that was it. Within an hour of me being home, this man called my mother's house 10 times. My mother asked me who he was and where I met him? I had a lot of explaining to do. Once I finally took the call, he asked if he could see me later that evening. I was going back outside anyway. That is what we did back then. Going outside to meet friends was better than social media.

He met me half-way and we hung out at the park and talked for a few hours. My mom got upset because she did not know where I was. Once I got home, I settled in and went to sleep. The next morning, this man called me about twenty times from the morning to the afternoon. My mother asked me if there was something wrong with him? I told her that he seemed nice. At this point, I only knew him for less than 24 hours.

The next day I decided to go to the movies with my best friend. He told me that he did not want me to go. Mind you, I had only known him for less than 24 hours at this point. Because I am strong willed, I went out that evening anyway with my friend. As I arrived home, he was standing in front of my stoop waiting for me. My mother said he had been there for six hours. Because I was young, I was unsure how to register this type of behavior. To be honest, I did not know we were in a committed relationship. After all, I had only known him for 24 hours at this point.

In two weeks, he said he loved me. He gave me flowers and cards every day. One day, I told him that I did not want to sleep over at his house. He then proceeded to call me a "fat bitch."

I was blindsided and confused. If I did something that he did not like, then the incessant phone calls would stop. He would give me the silent treatment as a form of punishment. As time went on, he continued to talk down to me about my weight. One day I was eating a hamburger and he told me *"If you keep eating like that, then you will be big as a house."*

The verbal abuse began slowly and then escalated. I could not understand how a person can say they love you one minute, and then degrade you verbally the next. After nine months, I broke up with him. I could not take the constant degrading of my character any longer.

Surprisingly, 10 years later, I saw him while I was out shopping. He was obese at this point. He looked me up and down and told me he could not believe I was no longer fat. I could have made him feel bad about his weight, but I decided to be the bigger person. As time went on, I continued to attract the same type of man in my life. It would feel like I was dating the same man, but in a different body. I could not understand why this continued to happen to me.

Each man would all have the same traits and characteristics. Once I gave my life to the Lord, God started to show me that we attract what we are. Yes, the Law of Attraction is real. Some people use the Law of Attraction to gain material wealth. The Law of Attraction can be used in other areas of your life as well.

God revealed to me that I never cleared my life from the first guy at the age of eighteen and that is why I continued to attract the same type of man. When people become sexually entangled, a soul tie is created. Before moving on, there are spiritual steps that should be taken to break the soul tie.

If the soul tie is not broken, then a person will continue to attract the same type of person in their lives. If the soul is broken or still tied to someone else, the result will only lead to meeting someone like yourself who is also broken. After reading books about the Law of Attraction and the Word of God, I was now ready to break free from this cycle. God gave me the revelation on the spiritual steps to break free.

Positioned for Change

Change is inevitable when your mindset matches the desired direction that you want to go. In order to change your outer world, you must change your inner world. The following steps were downloaded to me by the Holy Spirit based on Biblical principles to bring a transformational change to my situation.

Once you heal from the inside, the Law of Attraction will begin to work on your behalf. You will begin to attract what you are, healed and whole instead of broken and depressed. God allowed me to transform my inner world to attract not only the right relationships but bring Divine connections to fulfill my destiny:

1. **No Contact and Walk Away:** In order to successfully move forward, the first step is to walk away. When I went no contact, I did not look back. I had to block and delete from the cell phone, social media outlets, and avoid all personal interactions.

2. **Forgiveness:** I had to forgive myself for opening the door to an emotional abuser. God is so gracious that He did not want me to walk around with that heavy burden on my life. I also had to forgive the emotional abusers that I allowed in my life. Once I forgave, new doors of opportunity opened for me. God commands us to forgive, as He has forgiven us. I used the model prayer that Jesus outlined as a reminder:

"Our Father in heaven, Hallowed be Your name. Your kingdom come. Your will be done On earth as it is in heaven. Give us this day our daily bread. And forgive us our debts, As we forgive our debtors. And do not lead us into temptation, But deliver us from the evil one. For Yours is the kingdom and the power and the glory forever. Amen." (Matthew 6:8-13 NKJV)

3. **Prayer:** Seek the Lord in prayer. In order to successfully move forward, I had to spend time in God's presence. The time I spent with the Lord allowed me to receive prophetic downloads, Divine direction, and deliverance. I had a healing in my mind that only God can do. The Holy Spirit is also a comforter. God covered me in His blanket of love, as I moved forward into my promised land of mental peace and breakthrough.

4. **Fasting:** God instructed me to go on multiple fasts. My favorite fast is the 40 day fast with no food and drink only water from 6:00 a.m. – 6:00 p.m. During the time of fasting, God caused soul ties

to break off my life. I begin to see heavy burdens lifted and chains broken. In order to break stubborn soul ties, fasting along with prayer, causes heavy burdens to break. There are some dark forces that can only be broken and removed from your life through a fast.

"However, this kind does not go out except by prayer and fasting."
(Matthew 17:21)

5. **Praise and Worship**: I listened to praise and worship music during my prayer time. The presence of God was ushered into my situation. All soul wounds were healed, and deliverance sprang forth. When King Saul's spirit was distressed, he called upon David to play the harp. Music shifts the atmosphere to usher in a breakthrough.

"And so, it was, whenever the spirit from God was upon Saul, that David would take a harp and play it with his hand. Then Saul would become refreshed and well, and the distressing spirit would depart from him." (1 Samuel 16:23)

6. **Seek Professional Help**: In the Black community, going to a therapist for psychological support is not something that is well spoken of. In order to seek wholeness, it is a good idea to mix spiritual tools along with medical and/or professional psychiatric help. The brain is an organ. Just as your other organs need to be maintained, the brain also needs attention. Once I found a good therapist, I was able to be successful in my healing journey.

7. **Positive Associations**: I began to connect with people who were moving in the direction of life that I desire to be. One factor to begin to attract what you want, is to be in the atmosphere of what

you desire. If you are hurt, then you will attract other hurt people who will introduce you to broken and abused men and friends.

In my case, I surrounded myself with women who were focused on building themselves up in the Lord. I rededicated my life back to the Lord and surrounded myself with those in my faith community. Once I realized my worth, I valued the type of relationships that I wanted in my life. Birds of a feather flock together.

8. **Declarations**: God began to teach me how to decree a thing so it shall be established unto me. When you encounter a narcissistic person, the use of abusive words will linger in the mind. God's Word is powerful. Daily, I constructed my own declarations from the Word of God. For example: **"I am beautiful, God created me in His Divine image and likeness."**

A stronghold is a mental belief that is created in the mind. Strongholds can only be dismantled by using the Word of God. A new belief system needs to be created in order to attract new healthy relationships.

9. **Visualization**: I started to see myself only attracting emotionally healthy people. I began to uplift my inner vibration by using my imagination to see only healthy and whole people coming into my life.

10. **Learn to Love Yourself**: Do you know who you are? I learned to love myself even more. If you have spent your life around other people all the time, then how do you ever know what you want in life. I spent time getting to know who I really am as a person. I learned how to love myself as Christ loves the church. God taught me to love myself in order to move forward. If you have certain

issues that you do not like, then begin to love the flaws and begin to make them better. That was a great lesson for me.

11. **Self-Care**: God gave me the instruction to take care of myself. I began to do things that made me personally happy. When you continue to do things that make others happy and neglect yourself, you will feel a sense of emptiness. I go to the spa and enjoy time alone getting to know myself. I spend time at home doing facials and pedicures. I love to travel. I also enjoy aroma therapy. Reading books is also therapeutic. In my opinion, self-care is anything that makes you personally happy.

12. **The Power of No**: Listen, this is one of the most freeing steps. If you do not want to do something, then say NO. The power of telling someone no in a situation that I did not want to partake in, brought liberation to my soul. In this society, people think they must show up to every event, support everyone, and give unworthy people money. The biggest lesson I learned was to know when to say no without feeling guilty.

When you learn the power of telling someone no, you take back your personal power in the name of Jesus! Remember you are now creating a new life. Do not let others create your life for you. Do not become another person's slave.

"Do you not know that to whom you present yourselves slaves to obey, you are that one's slaves whom you obey, whether of sin leading to death, or of obedience leading to righteousness?" (Romans 6:16)

SOURCES

https://psychcentral.com/lib/
narcissistic-abuse-affects-over-158-million-people-in-the-u-s#1

https://www.mayoclinic.org/diseases-conditions/
narcissistic-personality-disorder/symptoms-causes/syc-20366662

FROM SILENCE
TO SELF-LOVE

Erica Nobles

I am a small-town girl with big dreams to change the world. I have worked for Fortune 500 companies in a customer-centric capacity and helped others to promote and grow their businesses. I am now preparing to launch my own business. I have been a "Jack of all Trades" for everyone else but have now chosen to focus on being the master of my own for myself. I am choosing me. In choosing myself, I am actively working towards achieving my dreams and goals. The only person who has more say so than me, is God.

Silent Suffering

Studies show that people fear speaking up because they truly fear rejection. It is a part of our innate nature to want to belong to something bigger than ourselves. And from an anthropological stance, we have a better chance of survival if we are in a group. Being alone is the equivalent of death. If speaking up means we will be left alone to die, then we will stay and suffer in silence. Even if that silence is also killing us.

My life has taught me that suffering in silence is a slow and painful death. Also, an unnecessary one. Although we naturally crave companionship and the safety of belonging to a group, that is sometimes the thing that is destroying us. Most of us have been taught that something is better than nothing, and to be grateful for what we have. Those statements are true. But we must also learn and instill, to never become so grateful for something, that we settle for less than what God said we should have. Come with me on my journey of self-discovery, and see how I went from suffering in silence, to loving myself out loud.

Born Into Love

I come from a rather unique background. I was born in a small town when my parents were 18 years old. My mom saw my dad as her everlasting love. My dad saw my mom as something to enjoy. When they broke up, my mom and I lived with my grandparents. It was me, my mom, my grandparents, two aunts, and two cousins. Me, one of the aunts, and both cousins were all within a year of each other in age, so we were more like sisters for a while.

My poor grandpa, he was the only male in that house. Did I forget to mention that we only had one bathroom? You can never tell me that he did not love his family, to put up with all of us women and girls. My grandparents both lost their parents when they were young. That made them fine with having a house full of loved ones.

About a mile or two down the road and around the corner, were my father's parents. I had them too. Along with more aunts, uncles, and cousins. The cousins were girls, also within my age range. I did not realize for years that this grandmother was my father's stepmother. I only knew that they were my family. I was never treated any differently and did not feel left out. I knew that I was loved. And I loved them back.

I was not treated as an outsider or called a "step" anything. I was a daughter, granddaughter, niece, and cousin. That was it. Most people were divided by their families, with words and phrases used to separate and differentiate this one from that one, and this group from that group. But not for me. I just was. To be loved and accepted on every side is beautiful and rare.

Childhood Silence

As time progressed, my mom and I moved away to a larger city and I left my childhood home behind. Once in the new location, I made new friends, or so I thought. I did not realize how mean and cruel, children can be. I went from being one of the group, to the odd one out.

I stopped being asked to play, was not invited to people's houses or birthday parties, and no one would talk to me in school. Not to mention the lies they told about me. I did not know what happened or when it happened, but I accepted it and continued with my day-to-day life, without friends of course. The resiliency of childhood is amazing. But that was the start of a terrible pattern of ignoring my pain and pretending to be OK, when I was not.

My mother was a woman who was popular, so she did not understand why I was having so many issues with keeping friends. But I was an introvert by nature so spending time alone was nothing unusual. I always liked to read and was fine playing by myself, so I drew further into that. The good news in all of this was that the districts were rezoned for my neighborhood and I ended up going to a different school. There I met new kids. I fit in so much better and was given a much-needed break from the other things. I got to be a regular kid again.

Transitional Silence

Not too long after that, we had to move back home. I missed my new friends, but I missed my family too. I was ready to go back and be with them again. And it went from relief to dread. Everyone had matured a little faster than me, so I was not included in much. Some people tried and were nice to me. I was the girl that would rather read and do schoolwork, put all my long, thick hair into a ponytail, and "talked white."

I was not into sports or boys, and not always getting my hair and nails done. I once went to a basketball game and read a book in the bleachers. I wanted to read a book and listen to music that was not only played on the R&B stations. Those were my outlets from the expectations that I was supposed to be someone I was not.

To make my life easier, I learned to disappear. I did not go to the movies or the hang out spots. I did not invite people to my house or go to theirs. My activities with my classmates were limited to school. I was not invited and did not want to go where I was not wanted. But as soon as I could, I got away and went home. I had a few friends that made things easier, but for the most part I was good being alone.

Fighting Silence

The most memorable situation I had is the one where I went through my first domestic violence experience in ninth grade. This was with a boy that really liked me. It was not mutual. He had asked me out several times and each time I said no. Me being polite and respectful in declining, coupled with his idea that perseverance and diligence would cause me to change my mind, was a recipe for disaster.

He did not seem to see me as an actual human being, just some objective, so my "nos" were not heard or respected by him. To confirm this, he decided to literally corner me one day. I had gotten to class early and no one else was in there. I was at my desk at the end of the row with a bookcase that spanned the entire wall behind me. When I saw him come in, I knew something bad was coming. I got up to walk out of the room and he rushed to get in front of me and blocked me. I tried to go around him, and he moved with me and then went to touch me.

That pissed me off! I pushed him away and went to walk around him. Next thing I knew, he was choking me. Then the teacher came back in. She ran out and came back in with help. They broke us apart and we each went to the principal's office. My mother left work to come and pick me up and he was suspended for a few days, but I was back in class the next day.

When he came back to class, he came to me and apologized for his behavior. And I did what we are supposed to do. I forgave him. I said nothing about what he did to me or let him, or anyone, know how I truly felt about the situation. I said and demanded nothing. It was over, so my thoughts were, let's get back to pretending to get along.

After all, when I came back to school, no one asked me how I was doing or if I was, OK? They actually made fun of me and it was the running joke because it's what I deserved. No counselor ever tried to talk to me, and it was not required that I speak to one. No police officer came to ask me if I wanted to press charges or get a restraining order. This was to be swept under the rug all to go on as if nothing happened. It was OK for me to be abused and my safety and wellbeing disregarded because it was too much of a bother.

Silent Burdens

My mother and I never talked about it. I remember pretending to be OK and going on with my life, as usual. I say pretending because that is what my life was at that time. One huge pretense, whatever is needed to get to and through the next day.

I was so used to pushing my thoughts and feelings down that I did not know how to acknowledge, let alone speak them. She was an overworked and underpaid single mother. This was something else for her to have to worry about. She had lost pay to come see about this. I would deal with it, so as not to cause an even bigger burden on her.

No More Silence

The fight at school was my turning point. When I was silent, I was treated unfairly and when I fought back, I was treated unfairly. Therefore, I decided to put myself first. I changed because if I was going to go through that type of hell for standing up for myself, then I should at least enjoy my life. And the issues they had were not mine, but theirs.

Somewhere between that fight and graduation, I decided to live for myself and not others. I couldn't control what others did, so I decided to create the life I wanted. I did not change because of anyone other than myself. I was able to face, address, and overcome all of this, by learning to recognize and appreciate what makes me different. Those differences are what makes me strong. I learned to love myself. To do that I had to make some changes.

1. I hung out more and attended some events.

2. I spoke up and ended up with some good memories.

3. I acknowledged that not everyone is worthy of what I have to offer.

4. I have learned to set boundaries, but not constantly reinforce them. The need for constant reinforcement means that my voice is intentionally being ignored because it is not convenient for someone else, with no regard for me. That relationship has to be limited if not ended completely.

5. I have learned that I owe no one anything. I choose to be me because that is who God designed me to be. He is the author and the finisher, not me, and certainly not them.

6. I have also learned that I can say no, without an explanation. I do not owe it, and they are not entitled to have it.

This has truly given me the freedom to be accepting and loving of myself. I always remember that I would rather be alone and happy, than coupled and miserable. The person who walks alone is usually the strongest one. Being accepted into a crowd is easy. Standing tall in the face of adversity is difficult, but how else will you know how strong you are?

Crowds and people disappear. You will always have yourself. And for that reason alone, you should like yourself. I want the same for you as well. So be strong, stand tall, and look them in their eyes, and without flinching, simply say, "I like me and that is more than enough."

Choose to Love

My life started out with me being loved and that's how I chose it to be now. I'm loving myself more and more. I want you to apply and remember this for your life. I want you to be so in love with yourself, that no one can tell you that you deserve less than the best. I want you to know your value and recognize that your strength is sometimes an indication of someone else's weakness.

I want you to be comfortable being the wonderful, marvelous, intelligent, talented, gifted, loving, kind, compassionate, and amazing individual you were created to be. I want you to look in the mirror each day and be absolutely in love with you. Because you are worth it, and darling, you do so deserve it.

ESCAPING POVERTY WHILE CULTIVATING POWER

Orjanette Bryant

Have you discovered the challenges of escaping the generational curse of lack, brokenness, and poverty? Poverty can lead you behind those metallic bars full of malodorous existence; I was tired of being financially, spiritually, and socially broken. Robbing Peter to pay Paul was like a nightmare rehearsed in my mind. I was headed nowhere, and I was desperate for a change. Come along with me as I uncover my path to success.

Children may grow up in poverty, but that doesn't stop them from pursuing their dream. Living the dream is the ultimate hustle. I overcame poverty, mental abuse, sexual assault, and childhood bullying. I transitioned from an impoverished youth to a successful medical professional, published author, mother, business owner, and financial literacy consultant.

My mission is to help others transform pain, shame, and guilt into a mission of purpose. Recovering and discovering is an ongoing journey, I know because my trauma nearly cost me everything, including my family. My recovery required God to heal me from the residual feelings of shame, worthlessness, and insecurity. However, I remember a counselor informing me that my experience would affect my future and my relationships.

Consider the Old Testament story of Lodebar. Lodebar was a low place, reminiscent of a "ghetto," in our current times. I was determined to put all the trauma behind me.

As an adult, I discovered a generational interruption into my spiritual path. My great-great-great grandfather's native land ritual and my Pentecostal upbringing caused some spiritual conflict in my life and my ability to process the balance of me as a black woman alone, educated, strong, and independent.

Poverty

According to the U.S. Census Bureau, over 30% of American single home families are experiencing poverty, (U.S. Census Bureau, 2005). Poverty is not limited to below financial means it is a mindset. This is a mindset that must shift. *Merriam-Webster* defines, "**Poverty as a lack of socially acceptable amount of money or possession, scarcity, dearth, malnourishment, and lack of fertility, and renunciation as a member of a religious order forfeiting their right to own property.**" "Renunciation of a religious leader" seems far-fetched. However, I believe I must add that more religious bodies of believers understand the concept of giving and they believe that if they live according to the Bible, then they are serving their purpose on Earth.

I define poverty as a curse that has been passed down from generation to generation. And yet I believe it can be broken. We can free ourselves from the prison it puts us in, emotionally. Most American families are stuck into a paycheck-to-paycheck mentality or cycle; they work multiple jobs to get by. Spending every dime on the latest name brand to conceal the fact that they often do not have enough to purchase a home or even make a car payment.

My Escape From Poverty

My family heritage begins in Quitman, Georgia, a land that was poorly governed with a low population. In my mind, the reason it had little to no regulations or governance was that the leader and founder were too busy serving the Mexican-American War. I would go visit Quitman annually and listen to the stories of how my family evolved. One of those stories was that my grandmother moved to the place known as, "The World's Most Famous Beach," Daytona Beach, Florida to accept a job working in the production industry. Daytona is known for race cars, bike week, and spring break. I thought I was special because my dad participated in the races, with his flashy red Kawasaki

Ninja. We had everything we needed; we lived in a home, although the rental property was rat-infested and poorly structured. I did not know we were poor and struggling like everyone else.

Daytona's average income was $20,000 and some people are complacent with the financial restrictions and have no problems sending their children to college to increase the debt. We were taught wrong. That native curse was to escape slavery to be free and broke. My family did not invest in their own land or property, although my grandmother took the leap and learned that she could, and she would do much better than her ancestors. She was not going to owe any man anything, nor was she going to limit her existence to an internal prayer to the land that was stolen.

My family made sure I knew how to swim. Trust me. I learned about God early because I had a close encounter with death in that deep blue sea. I found myself trying to understand things at a young age and asking my best friend, Granny for guidance along the way. My mom was quite submissive, and she worked at a local department store, while my Dad worked for the city, he had a Buick and rode a motorcycle. When I started elementary school, my nightmares began. I was alone mostly and sheltered. As the oldest grandchild, I was taught to pray to God. Once the bullying began, my mother influenced me to turn the other cheek. I turned the other cheek until I began to wonder who I was? Mom kept reminding me that I was a child of God.

The idea of being a child of God and living like Jesus was tough for me to process. Because I was gifted in art, I began to create my imaginary world with my artistic talent. I was commissioned by my first-grade teacher, Mr. Evans to do an African shield for the casements in the home of John Rockefeller that was to be displayed in Ormond Beach. I was so poor, going to the home of the richest man in modern history was not even a part of my thoughts.

Today, I drive past the casements; however, I have never had the privilege of seeing them in person, although my artwork won a great honor of second place during the art exhibit. My art teacher believed in me at the age of five and he stirred in me inspiration and hope, but that moment only lasted for a short time. The rest of my educational years became a nightmare when a teacher decided she was going to suppress my ability to learn. I felt like a slave. Blacks were not able to read or write and I at the age of six could only accept what was given to me at that time.

As I grew older, I began to comprehend deceptions and dysfunction, and as a result, I required therapy. During group therapy at the age of 12, I silently listened to other sexual assault victims as they shared taking their power back from a life of prolonged pain into prostitution, sex, and drugs. Stuck in my innocence, yet traumatized, I wanted a family and I wanted to escape the harm that had been done to me, so I sought God for an escape outside of my deepest pain.

One of the other lessons I learned is that I needed to be tough and take my power back. Thank God my step dad taught me self-defense and even how to hold a gun and use it if necessary. There are parts of Daytona that are full of violence. I lived only five miles from the corner store where the prostitutes hang out. This was the same area where the female serial killer was killing men who paid for sexual services. Those streets were not frightening to me.

Transformation

My defining moment was when the cops came to get me at school after a fight. Because of the nature of the fight, I had to go to court. The judge wanted to take me away from my mother and we had to go through great measures so that that was not the case. I was forced to serve my community.

This Journey Is for You

There are many young men and women who found a resolution to deal with the generational curses of poverty. We as a people forget how powerful we are. Learning to accept our strength and gaining access to a much bigger world is ultimately the reason I wanted to take you on this journey with me. I know a lot of street-smart people, and I know surviving the streets is in your control; however, my message of hope is to inspire you to accept the challenge and get past the pain of poverty. Letting go of the disruptive path in the streets is critical for your existence.

Brothers and sisters, you do not have to allow the streets to determine your destination. You must tell yourself you can, and no matter how hard it gets, you will succeed. Prison is no different than slavery or the drugs that destroy our health; you must take control of the power from within you. I escaped the trail of tears and I refused to allow being broken to define my story. I will leave a legacy for the new generation and I am determined to experience that transformation of abundance and overflow.

Post Pandemic Crisis

The Global Bank shares statistics that poverty is expected to rise over the next 20 years and with the COVID-19 pandemic, it may even cost us all a price bigger than our existence. Unfortunately, the projection of the post COVID-19 pandemic 2020, 88 million to 115 million people will be pushed to extreme poverty, bringing the total somewhere between 729 to 793 million. 1 out of 10 people in the world lives off less than $1.90 a day. I remember sending money to Africa to support education and what if we donated just $3 a day to support other families in need of food, medical care, and housing. We can make a difference and support each other, globally. We fight over nothing although we have access to plenty.

My Tips for Escaping Poverty

1. Growing Spiritually

2. Investing in training

3. Going to school

4. Getting a mentor and a life coach

5. Dreaming big and defining who I wanted to be

6. Telling myself I was great

7. Joining an investment group

8. Listening to powerful overcomers

9. I stopped spending so much time with family members who constantly remind me of my past

10. I joined groups with millionaire networks

11. I got training through SBA, or Score to support my entrepreneur spirit

12. I wrote the vision and made it plain

13. I understood that it takes $20,000 weekly to become a millionaire or increase your net worth

14. I stopped socializing with dream killers

15. I spent less and saved more

16. I didn't allow narcissism or gas-lighters to be the ammunition to minimize my potential

17. Freed myself, forgave, let go, and let God!

Rethinking Poverty

Today, I am a published author, a nurse practitioner, a master's prepared college graduate, a business owner, and a woman of influence. In my journey, I stopped allowing others and their negative energy to influence my path. People often try to escape what poverty looks like, by wearing the latest and greatest. They often disguise the look by masking their skin with layers of make-up. Escaping insecurity is an ongoing challenge. Poverty is not cute, but society says you must look like you got it going on and pretend to have it all, even when multiple limitations hinder your growth. Words like cannot, will not, or refuse, are traps you must avoid.

Can't is a negative implanted concept we tell ourselves and we stick to the possibility of what that means.

Will not is an awful reality people or naysayers say watching others grow and prosper. They spend more time talking others into dreaming big and understanding the possibility, but many people refuse to take that leap of faith. Be mindful that mental entrapments are implanted in us all. The ID and ego play a major role in our subconscious thinking. Like my past painful abuse, it is easy to replay the same horrific trauma. The road to hell is not difficult to turn to, but once the flames from that fire hit your body, you must renavigate your path. You must tell yourself you can, you will, and be intentional about accomplishing it.

People who have been abused, mistrust others because they have a layer of unsolved pain and unforgiveness that makes them refuse to accept any challenge that feels remotely uncomfortable. Get out of the painful pitfall of the past and start to focus on a promising future. Think about your legacy and your children's children and how you must impact them. Rahab from the Bible most definitely left a legacy outside of her past occupation as a prostitute; she is the ancestor of Jesus and the first woman to ensure a path for an escape from poverty. Dreamers must be willing to take the plunge to see themselves outside of the pain that never defined them.

People look for validation in others and often never receive anything outside a painful past. Poverty is a mental, physical, and financial trap. This trap is often supported and influenced by others around us. It takes a lot of bravery to become an overachiever and step outside the familiar norms. People who make it do not necessarily look like they have arrived.

In my opinion, the millionaire mindset should be adopted. Identifying who you are, who you want to be, and where you want to go. The first thing required after the vision is clear is for you to develop, trust, and plan. It is time to escape the metaphoric analogy of the rats climbing up the same curtain used to dress you.

Empowerment After Changes & Losses

"Real change, enduring change, happens one step at a time."- Ruth Bader Ginsburg

FROM BLIND TO WOKE

Felicia Butler

C an you imagine waking up from your fairytale dream to living your worst nightmare? Sometimes we see through our heart, but when we finally open our eyes, what we thought we had, is not what it turns out to be. I wanted what most women want-to fall in love, get married, and have children. I had my wedding planned out in my mind ever since I was a young girl and how wonderful life would be. Everything seemed to be going in the right direction.

I fell in love and got married. I had no idea what I was getting into. I thought he was perfect. The side I saw was. There was another side, though. The side he didn't want me to see struggled to overcome a secret past. This is a glimpse of my journey from being blind to woke after unknowingly falling into a mixed orientation relationship.

Mixed Orientation Relationships

There are many reasons why there are mixed orientation relationships. In 2013, there was a study conducted by Iowa University about this. The results of the study discovered that the most popular reason we remain in mixed orientation relationships is because of love. Other reasons are believing that marriage will lessen the desires for the same sex (Corley & Kort, 2006).

Some couples were young and not fully aware of what their sexual orientation was until after they were married and realized that they were forcing being heterosexual (Higgins, 2002). In most cases, the spouses were unaware that their partner was having sexual orientation issues. Some did report that they were told shortly before marriage, (Yarhouse, Pawlowski, & Tan, 2003).

Family or societal pressure was another reason. Among a highly religious sample, it was mutual with both partners who reported feeling like marriage was the right thing to do. Being in love, wanting children, and a family life were the most common reasons for marrying, (Yarhouse, Pawlowski, & Tan, 2003).

I do not know what my husband's reasons were. I did not get the opportunity of having that open and honest conversation before I married him. That part of his life was kept from me. There were signs. I ignored them. There are up to two million mixed-orientation couples. When the gay, lesbian, or bisexual partner comes out, most do not stay together. In my case, I did not have to deal with a split up or divorce, the unthinkable happened.

My Family

I grew up in a traditional household. I was raised in a two-parent family. I have four brothers and I am the youngest and only girl. My father was in the military and I was born outside of the United States in Seville, Spain. We moved from there when I was five to Zweibrücken, Germany. We were there for about a year.

After that deployment, my father came back to the United States and was stationed at Whiteman Air Force Base in Missouri. He was there until he retired. When he retired, he moved us to Columbia, Missouri. I was eight-years-old. I was close to my father.

He formed my idea of what a husband should be like-a good provider and a strong disciplinarian. He was military strict on all of us. When I was of dating age, his rules for dating were so strict that there was no one who could meet those standards. I was "saved," so of course that young man had to be "saved" among the other things my dad added. So, I did not date until I was in college.

My First Boyfriend

After I graduated from high school, I continued my education at the University of Missouri in Columbia and majored in Nursing. I started hanging around the college students that attended my church. I was involved in the campus ministry and joined the church's campus gospel ensemble. There was a young man that was a few years older than me that was the piano player for the campus choir, and he also played the organ at our church. I had a crush on him.

He had been going to our church ever since he started at the university, so I met him when I was around 16, but we never talked. That changed when one day he approached me as I was leaving the church and handed me a beautifully written Valentine's Day card. When I went home and read it, I could hardly sleep. He had confessed that he was interested in me and thought I was beautiful. Shortly after that, we became boyfriend and girlfriend with dad's approval of course because he was "saved."

Our relationship was extremely Christian. No sex. We only kissed a few times on dates. When he came over to the house, he sat on one side of the couch and I sat on the other. We had been dating for about a year when I asked him, "So when are we getting married?" He agreed that we should get married. He told me that he was wanting to ask me, but he felt I would say I wanted to wait, but I needed to get away from my super strict father. So, even though we did not have my parent's blessing, we moved forward with our wedding plans.

My Marriage

August 4, 1984, at 20-years-old, I got married. I was happy to get away from my overbearing father. That happiness changed to awkwardness by the next morning, though. I woke up still a virgin. When I saw the sun peeking through the bridal suite curtains, I realized I had fallen asleep before we could consummate our marriage. Neither one of us talked about it, but there was definitely an elephant in the room. We tried to be intimate that morning, but it was awful and painful.

From that moment forward, every attempt at intimacy was a bad experience. I thought it was me. I thought it was a combination of both of us being inexperienced. We continued on with our awkward in the bedroom marriage. Somehow, I managed to get pregnant three times. My first pregnancy ended in a miscarriage about six weeks into it.

My Suspicion

We had moved to Mississippi in 1992 for my husband to attend Bible college majoring in music. Our marriage was doing well in every aspect, except intimacy. I began to wonder if he was cheating. Many times, I woke up at night and he would be gone. I did not know when it started. When I realized he was leaving at night, I would lie in bed wide awake just to see what time he would get home.

Sometimes, it would be 2:00 am in the morning. Sometimes, 3:00 am in the morning. I would pretend I was asleep. He would quietly come in the house, get into his night clothes in the dark, and ease into bed being careful to not wake me up. One night after he got into bed, much to his surprise, I rose straight up, turned on the light, looked at him straight in the face, and confronted him about it.

His explanation was that he could not sleep sometimes, and he got up and went for rides. Sometimes he went to the 24-hour grocery store and read magazines. Although I did not believe it, I let it slide. Everything else about my life was good. Good job, two beautiful children, wonderful church, and he was a great father and always kept a job so I figured I should leave it alone.

The Truth Comes Out

In our 10th year of marriage, I noticed that he was having significant weight loss. He had suffered two bouts of, "walking pneumonia," thrush, continuing night sweats, and bothersome diarrhea. He was wasting away. I urged him to go get checked. He finally went to a doctor for some answers. I went with him two weeks later on his return visit. I was thinking he had cancer or a thyroid condition. Long story short, he was HIV-positive in full blown AIDS.

The night before the doctor's appointment where he would find out his diagnosis, he wrote me a letter, which he handed to me as the doctor pulled him out of the exam room to tell him his results. In the letter, he confessed what he had been hiding from me all those years, he had a gay past and he feared he had HIV. He explained how when he was in college before we started dating, he was in a homosexual relationship and received a call from the Columbia, Missouri Health Department telling him he was named as a sexual partner of someone who had a contagious disease and he needed to get his blood checked.

In the letter, he wrote that he went and got his blood drawn, but that whole experience scared him straight. He never went back for his results and tried to forget about it. That was in 1981. I started dating him in 1982 and we got married in 1984. In 1995, two days after his diagnosis, he began struggling to breathe and he passed away in the hospital from pneumocystis carinii pneumonia. I felt like I was in a small boat in the ocean with no sail or compass. I was scared, too.

What if he had given this to me? I had decided that if he had given me HIV, I was going to take my life and our children's life. I had a plan. I would have us go to sleep in my running car with the garage door down and my windows open and hopefully we would all die together from carbon monoxide poisoning.

The Miracle

Those were the darkest days of my life. There are no words that can adequately describe the feelings of hopelessness knowing I had been exposed to HIV for 10 years. I needed to get tested, but first I had to have a serious talk with God. It went something similar to this- "God, you cannot let this happen. I have done everything right. I have lived for you the best I know how, and You have to not let me have this."

At that moment, I experienced what felt like hot oil being poured on my head and went down my body. Through tear-filled eyes I had to look down at my body because it was so tangible. I truly believe I was being healed right then. Prior to this day, I was having some of the same symptoms my husband had. I had been losing weight. I was having diarrhea and night sweats. So, I went all alone to get tested. I was scared to death of what the results might be.

When I went back for my results, I was still alone. My heart was pounding, and I held my breath as I was being told my results. It was negative. I knew there was a window period where HIV is undetectable so I kept getting tested and sweating it out every time until I would get my result. On the 8th time and after several months of getting tested, I finally was convinced I did not have HIV. I was going to live.

Getting My Life Back

I moved back to Columbia. I had a new appreciation for life and promised myself I would no longer take anything for granted, but I also realized I needed healing for my damaged spirit. I felt I could not talk about the ordeal I had gone through, so I held it all in. My pastor at the time and others in the church kept telling me to have faith and that everything was going to be fine. Little did they know, they did not have the full truth. I was not telling most how he really died. Most thought he died suddenly of normal pneumonia, not HIV pneumonia. All I had to cling on to was my belief that God would bring me through and even though that got shaky at times, I was not about to think that God was going to let me down.

Getting Help

Looking back, there are things that I did not do that would have helped me. The Bible tells us in:

"Without counsel purposes are disappointed: but in the multitude of counselors they are established." (Proverbs 15:22)

After my husband died, I should have gotten counseling right away. I robbed myself of guidance and the release of emotions by holding it all in. I needed to talk about it. I did not know how to do that. I prayed for strength because I was taught to take everything to God. I did eventually receive counseling, but a few years had passed.

Prayer kept me sane, but the counseling helped me put things in proper perspective. I have learned how to open up. In retrospect, I have learned from all of this, not only to seek good counsel, but also not to ignore the red flags. My advice to singles before marriage is:

1. Have no secrets with each other.

2. Get pre-marital counseling.

3. Be true to yourself. If you know you are having sexual orientation issues, then you are not ready for marriage.

4. For people who have a loved one about to get married, if you do not have good vibes or you know something about their significant other that you know could make a difference, then tell them.

Life Is Good Again

With my faith in God and counseling, which helped me to gradually open up, I got through the most difficult time of my life. I have grown a lot. I found love again. I have been able to get back to the semblance of the happy, trusting woman I used to be. I went back to school and received my master's degree in Nursing and presently work as a Nurse Practitioner, Online Instructor, and a Preceptor for Nurse Practitioner students. Life is about choices. The choices we make today determine our tomorrows, but as the saying goes, today is the first day of the rest of your life. Choose wisely.

Bibliography

Gay Men from Heterosexual Marriages Attitudes, Behaviors, Childhood Experiences, and Reasons for Marriage Daryl J. Higgins PhD Pages 15-34 | Published online: 12 Oct 2008

Intact Marriages in which One Partner Dis-Identifies with Experiences of Same-Sex Attraction.

Yarhouse, Mark A.; Pawlowski, Lisa M.; Tan, Erica S. N. American Journal of Family Therapy, v31 n5 p375-94 Oct-Dec 2003

Resilient Factors in Mixed Orientation Couples: Current State of the Research

Jill L. Kays &Mark A. Yarhouse Pages (334-343 | Published online: 07 Jul 2010

The Sex Addicted Mixed-Orientation Marriage: Examining Attachment Styles, Internalized Homophobia and Viability of Marriage After Disclosure. Sexual Addiction & Compulsivity,

Corley, M. D., & Kort, J. (2006). 13(2-3), 167–193.

WHEN PAIN
BIRTHS PURPOSE

Beatrice Charles

We've been trained to see predators like wolves so much so that it is almost impossible to see that the "gentle" shepherd can pose a greater threat to the flock. Have you ever met someone who appeared so harmless, as if they couldn't even kill a fly? As you get to know them, you realize they were a wolf in sheep's clothing. However, you missed the signs.

Domestic abuse is not limited to physical abuse, it's a broad spectrum of abuse. The narcissist is verbally, mentally, sexually, psychologically, and financially abusive due to their compulsive, addictive, and controlling personalities. Some narcissistic people are mild-mannered and are often undetected because they are passive-aggressive in nature. In the beginning, you'll think you've met the love of your life, but not so!

Narcissistic People

Approximately 0.5% of the U.S. population or 1 out of 200 people suffer from Narcissistic Personality Disorder (NPD). The purpose of me sharing my story is to help others identify the signs, behaviors, and red flags that I wasn't aware of. Some of the common symptoms of a narcissist include arrogant behavior, use, and exploit others, lack of empathy, sense of entitlement, a lust for power and success, obsessed with their appearance, self-image, need for constant admiration, and grandiosity, (making themselves appear impressive).

People with narcissistic personality disorder spend a significant amount of time comparing themselves to others. They desire to be in high positions in their careers or religious groups. They are willing to do anything to get ahead and are natural con artists. Some individuals with this condition consider themselves to be superior to others. People with NPD may be highly resistant to criticism or highly sensitive to perceived slights. Like other types of personality disorders, they tend to have other mental health conditions, including depression, anxiety, bipolar disorder, substance abuse, gambling addiction, or compulsive behavior.

My Run-In With Narcissism

Let me take you on my journey of how I was in what I like to call a "hit and run." In the beginning, he came into my life seemingly out of nowhere, and coincidentally it's the same way he left. I was totally blind-sighted. It all began one Sunday afternoon.

I noticed him staring at me and my children as we made our way into the church. He did not approach me right away, but about five months later, he slid into my DM and invited me to attend an out-of-town church event with him. About a week later, I was immediately being inundated with attention and adoration, to the point where it was overwhelming. As an unsuspecting empath, who has been sexually molested, raped, rejected, and abandoned as a child, I had no clue what a healthy pattern and flow of a relationship should look like. I was quickly swept off of my feet, with nice dinners and frequent flower deliveries.

I've since learned this is typical textbook behavior of a narcissist. It's the love bombing stage. It worked, hook, line, and sinker. Narcissistic people tend to marry quickly, particularly if you fit the mold of what they are trying to accomplish at that moment. My narcissist was a single father with an active young daughter. I had two slightly older children. We were both overwhelmed and it made sense to marry him. We were married 100 days later.

Almost immediately after our wedding, the mask started coming off little by little. He began to isolate me and my children from our close friends. He wanted everything to accommodate and revolve around him and his daughter. He began to brainwash my son by telling him that single mothers often resent their children. He would keep him up into the wee hours of the morning, having long private discussions in my son's bedroom.

I wasn't aware of the mental trauma he inflicted on him until we were separated. Did I mention that we were pastoring a church during all of this? The first year I tried to ignore his constant lying, verbal, and financial abuse, manipulation, silent treatment, neglectful ways, and triangulation of our family. (Narcissists attempt to control the flow, interpretation, and nuances of communication).

After depleting me of over $30,000 due to his gambling, reckless spending, and a drinking problem, the turning point for me was when he offered to get my son marijuana *if he ever wanted to try it*. I could no longer ignore the detriment this man was to me as well as my children. I asked him for a divorce, in hopes that he would make some necessary changes.

I went to our pastor requesting he meet with us. Shockingly, he asked me if I had been molested, as if to insinuate that I was "damaged goods." He later apologized for that incident that took place in his office and at the altar in the church that same Wednesday evening. I was not aware that my husband began to devalue me behind my back with some of our friends, his family, and most likely my pastor too. Hence his hurtful response because a person with NPD can't help but blame others for their mistakes.

He secretly recorded our heated conversations and played them with my teenage son. Telling him that when he leaves me, that I am to blame. God only knows who else heard those private conversations in which I had no idea that I was being recorded. Two and 1/2 years into our marriage, we agreed to be separated. He even suggested that I date other people. I now know this was a part of a sick narcissistic person's way of plotting for me to be publicly humiliated and take the blame for our pending divorce. Luckily for me, I had enough self-respect and dignity to not fall for such an asinine plot.

Overcoming Narcissistic Abuse

Immediately after my narcissist abruptly moved out of the house, I could feel the aftermath of the havoc he had been wreaking. My children had suffered from brainwashing and mind-control. A term the experts call *triangulation*. Triangulation is when a narcissistic person controls the narrative and flow of all conversations. I felt completely numb, broken, and confused. I knew that this was indeed the most difficult thing we had ever faced. I soon realized the full extent of his different personas.

There was no real person with actual feelings towards me or my children behind the many facades. Abusive people enjoy this framing game of destroying their victim's reputation. They provoke their chosen target for a reaction, then claim it as evidence of mental instability, evil-mindedness, or something else that implies it is the victim who is at fault. Diverting all attention away from his own behavior, the predator seeks support from others, turning them against his target.

It can be devastating for an individual who already is suffering from mistreatment to be blamed, slandered, rejected, and isolated. The narcissist enjoys the power and control he derives from tormenting with impunity and the positive attention he gets from playing the "victim" and fishing for sympathy from unsuspecting people. It is also an effective method of intimidating his or her target from attempting to speak up and expose the truth.

In a relationship, you or your children shouldn't have to think five steps ahead, walk on eggshells, anticipate their mood, take the blame for all tensions, read their mind, apologize for their behavior, and fear they may stop loving you from one day to the next. This isn't healthy love. It is control.

Narcissistic people covertly package themselves as love. Narcissists always play the victim, no matter how bad they've treated their victims. It's never about the verbal abuse, invalidation, criticisms, bullying, or cruel behaviors, but about the fact that you stood up to them and defended yourself. Narcissists can't stand it when their victims assert their rights because they think they are the only ones with rights. Hence, their sense of entitlement, power, and control.

Upon our separation, my narcissist blocked all forms of communication to me and my children with the exception of e-mail. This is called the discard, the narcissist way of getting rid of their supply and then moving on as if you never existed. Experts say this is another way they control their victims by making them feel inadequate and unworthy of even civil communication.

Blocking communication with their victims is their "go-to" to get out of the bad situations they've created and not take any responsibility. He used the silent treatment in order to avoid any responsibility for where we were. I felt numb experiencing what I had heard him tell me how he used to discard other people in his life. Now it was happening to me and my children. I think the only ones who could understand this type of abuse are people who have gone through it. Because if it didn't happen to me, I would have never accurately understood it.

It feels earth-shattering when the mask was completely off and he was so cold and cruel, almost gruesome at times. It is so difficult accepting that none of it was real. I felt traumatized all over again from my childhood. The rejection, abandonment, and public ridicule I faced left me shaken up. I thought I was going to have a nervous breakdown. I could not believe how he had fooled us all. Including the church. It was like waking up from a bad dream to a nightmare. He appeared so good, humble, kind, and compassionate in the beginning or whenever he wanted to be. It's so difficult getting used to the depths of his cruelty and ice-cold heart. The initial shock was not easy for me.

Once my children and I were alone again I had to decide how to navigate through this process. So, I decided to enroll us in family and individual counseling. In addition to that, I hired a life coach, which was truly life-transforming. My biggest breakthrough came when we began to work on my foundation, where it all began. I was sexually molested at the age of nine by my stepfather and raped at 12. I had never dealt with the trauma.

As a result of this, I made the wrong choices in identifying what love should look like. You see, I was determined to not allow this nightmare to haunt me or destroy our lives and destinies. I also developed a more in-depth relationship with my Lord and Savior, Jesus Christ. During that time of total isolation, through fasting and prayer, I learned of the call and demand He placed on my life. Nine months later, I birthed my call to ministry. My passion has always been single moms, who suffered trauma as I did.

I held my first annual ladies healing retreat on the ocean, complete with a therapist, my personal life coach, and a spiritual midwife. What an exhilarating time we had. The women who attended, laughed, cried, and left better than when they came. That's when I knew why God allowed the pain to come. Today, my children and I are rebuilding our lives, we are healthy and thriving.

Life After Narcissism

My marriage was necessary because it came with the "right" stuff to give me that thrust into my purpose and destiny. The things pivotal to me overcoming a narcissistic marriage were:

1. I was able to forgive myself because the deterioration of our marriage wasn't my fault.

2. During my therapy, I worked on becoming a better version of myself. I'm still an empath, that will never change, but now I am healed and whole.

3. I have mature boundaries and can recognize love through healthy lenses. My last relationship taught me a lot. It taught me not to ignore signs and my gut feeling.

4. I learned how to love myself and not put anyone above my happiness, goals, and dreams.

Now I know my worth, I know what I want and won't settle for less than we deserve ever again. I have no regrets. I needed to learn those life-transforming lessons and I am much better because of it ALL!

Bibliography

Mayo Clinic: https://www.mayoclinic.org/diseases-conditions/narcissistic-personality-disorder/symptoms-causes/syc-20366662

FROM DIVORCE AND DEPRESSION TO DESTINY

Katina Walker

Determined not to let it break me, I used it to make me stronger. I don't encourage divorce. In fact, I'm against it but it happens. If it happens to you, know that it's not the end of life for you, it will be what you make of it. Choose to make it the beginning of a bright new chapter. My goal is to enlighten divorced women with young children, to know that with the right thoughts and actions, they will not only survive, but they will also thrive in their new roles as a single woman and single parent.

The situation can be used to strengthen you and enable you to soar. Your mindset is a critical part of your outcome in such circumstances. Your success and happiness are in your mind, and you control it. It is important for women to not allow themselves to succumb to depression caused by divorce. Let me tell you how I defeated divorce's devastation.

In the United States, about 50% of all marriages end in divorce within the first 10 years of marriage. One in five women fall into poverty as a result of divorce. It has been estimated that about one in three women who own a home and have children at home when they divorce, lose their home. When getting married and planning a family, many are not prepared to handle the changes that can challenge the marriage. A study showed that 67% of couples reported a decline in relationship satisfaction after the baby arrives, typically between the 6th and 9th month.

Reference:https://www.wf-lawyers.com/divorce-statistics-and-facts/

The Root of the Problem

I grew up in a small town in Georgia. As a child, I struggled with fitting in with my family and my peers in school. My mom was 17 years old when I was born. She and my father never married and were not together long after I was born. I grew up with my mom's side of my family. Although it was a big family, marriage was not common. I felt as if I was an inconvenience to my mom and that having children was hard work for a parent.

Therefore, marriage and children were never a part of my dreams for my future. I wasn't raised in church. As a child, I only visited church occasionally when one of my aunts or my older cousin took me. I started going more frequent at the age of 19, when I was out on my own and trying to find myself.

In pursuit of more opportunities than my small hometown could offer me, I joined the US Army almost one year after I graduated high school. I served a four-year term in the Army stationed in Ft. Hood, TX. This is where I met my husband, he was also in the Army. Near the end of our military term, my mom was hospitalized, and my youngest sister was only nine years old, so I decided to move back to Georgia to be close enough to help out if needed.

My husband was thrilled about it because he was from Georgia as well, which meant, we would also be living close to his family. We moved to suburban Northeast Metro Atlanta. We were able to quickly get settled in and find jobs. We were doing well for ourselves as a young couple and were enjoying our lives together.

We were married for seven years when my husband asked me to have a baby. When I first met my husband, I told him I did not want to have children, and he agreed that if we were to get married, we would not have children. I felt stressed out and pressured, so I resisted his preposition to have a baby for a while. He became persistent, even stating that if I didn't have a baby, it meant I didn't love him.

In an effort to be a more submissive wife, I stopped resisting and agreed to have a baby. It didn't take long for me to get pregnant. I was sick during the first two trimesters. I felt that my husband wasn't there for me, as much as I needed him to be, during the times that I was sick. After the baby came, I felt my husband was not much involved in taking care of the baby and household duties. He would have a look of abandonment or neglect in his eyes. It upset me because prior to getting pregnant, I told him that it would be hard for me to do everything that I usually do for him and the household if I had a baby to take care of. Instead of helping out more, he became distant. After going through all of that, to grant my husband his wish, I was devastated to see that my marriage was ending after 10 years and he wasn't fighting for it, me, or our baby girl.

The Downward Spiral

He was always easily led by the wrong people. Now feeling that he wasn't getting all of the attention he wanted from me, he picked up bowling as a hobby. I thought it was great for him to now have a hobby. Unfortunately, this is where he met and connected with a guy who offered him a business opportunity that turned out to be a Ponzi Scheme. This caused us to have so much debt that we would never be able to pay it off. Shortly after figuring out that we were schemed and would not be getting any of the money back, my husband lost his job of eight years. He was happy with his job and I could only imagine the hurt he felt from losing it. Wanting to lift his spirits, I told him that everything would be ok. I encouraged him to look for another job. Each morning, I took our baby girl to daycare, and went to work feeling that he would use this time to search for another job.

On his birthday, I cooked his favorite dinner, bought a nice dessert and a birthday card, which I had our baby girl put her mark on. I placed her hand on the card while I traced it, then I wrote a special message from her in the drawing of her hand. My hope was that this would put a smile on his face, motivate him to get past the loss of his job, and move forward in finding a new one. He seemed to sink into depression. I initiated the interview for the first job he had so he expected me to do the leg work of helping him find another job, but with everything I had on my plate, I had no time to do so.

I could no longer afford to pay the mortgage on my income alone, so I asked him to call the mortgage company to see if they would work out an affordable plan. He told me that a representative from the mortgage company told him that we could pay half of the mortgage for the next six months, so that's what I did. However, we started receiving foreclosure notices and the mortgage company advised me that there was no such deal or plan put in place permitting us to only pay half of the mortgage. I became so frustrated with my husband not doing much to help with the household or the baby, that I asked him to leave. He went to stay with his cousin who lived less than three miles from our house.

I became so depressed that I started going through the motions, just enough to get through the day. I took our baby girl to daycare before I went to work each morning, picked her up after work, fed her, bathed her and put her and some of her toys in the bed with me so that she could play and watch TV while I rested until bedtime. I felt mentally and physically exhausted. I lost weight due to my lack of an appetite. At 32 years of age, I felt overwhelmed with having to be responsible for it all.

I suggested we go to marriage counseling, so I set up our appointments and we met with the therapist every week or two. However, being that he had started dating another woman, he felt conflicted. He expressed that he didn't want to hurt her because she was there for him when he felt alone. I was appalled that after all I had been for him as his wife, he was so arrogant about moving on with someone else. One night I had an overwhelming desire to talk to him, so I drove to his cousin's house. His car was in the driveway, but the house was dark, so I started to leave but seeing his car, my daughter started calling for him.

She was getting upset because she wanted to see him, so I went to the door and rang the doorbell. When he finally came to the door and let me and our baby girl in, I saw the girl that he was dating coming downstairs. Our daughter ran to her and then I realized that he had already introduced her to our little girl. She wouldn't allow him to talk to me long and he stood by her side, so I left feeling so much pain in my heart. I felt like going through divorce was the most devastating thing that I had to endure. I felt like a failure, the shame of feeling like I was becoming another statistic, divorced, single mom. I was so depressed that I spent the weekends with my sister so that she could help take care of my daughter while I slept most of the weekend away.

My sister started encouraging me to snap out of my depression. One weekend around my birthday, my neighbors kept my daughter to give me some time to rest. I was on my sofa, literally in a fetal position when I felt an urge to pick myself up and start reading the book that my sister bought me for my birthday. The book gave daily exercises for encouraging yourself through positive thinking. This was when my healing began.

Sunshine After the Rain

It took years of trials and soul searching for me to begin healing from divorce. It was overwhelming for me to balance working, taking care of a child, and household by myself while feeling so horrible about having a failed marriage, so I sought counseling.

1. Professional as well as spiritual counseling helped me tremendously. I first sought counsel from God, praying and crying out my frustrations while asking God to guide and provide. My therapist was awesome. She was also a woman of spiritual faith. The added bonus was that she could also relate to my circumstance from her own personal experience. Her story inspired me.

2. I started thinking positively about my situation, believing that I could still maintain my standard of living. Wanting to provide a comfortable life for my daughter, in spite of the divorce, was much of the fuel that drove me to act.

   "Just as the body is dead without breath, so also faith is dead without good works (action). (James 2:6)

3. I prayed and asked God to send people to help me during this most difficult time in my life. I wanted good people who I could trust to keep my daughter while I worked to provide our needs.

   "For everyone who asks, receives. Everyone who seeks, finds. And to everyone who knocks, the door will be opened." (Matthew 7:8)

I'm so grateful to my sister Donna, my bonus mom, my neighbors and some awesome friends, all of whom, the independent woman in me, had not thought to ask for help but was blessed by them volunteering to help. Between these wonderful people, I had someone to take care of my daughter while I took classes, put in extra hours at work, or needed a break.

4. There were struggles, we had to make sacrifices, my baby girl and I couldn't have or do some things we wanted, but all of our needs were still met, and I was able to save our home from foreclosure.

5. I was determined. I worked so hard and diligently that I was asked to take a higher position/promotion.

Colossians 3:23-24 (23) "Whatever you do, work at it with all your heart, as working for the Lord, not for human masters, (24) since you know that you will receive an inheritance from the Lord."

Fast forward six years later, after receiving a couple of promotions and performance bonuses from my job, my salary almost doubled. Then the job transitioned to work from home. This enabled me to save thousands on daycare or before and after school care, gas, wear and tear on my car, and other expenses. Trust in God, with all your heart, to be the provider that He says He is.

"And my God will meet all your needs according to the riches of his glory in Christ Jesus." (Philippians 4:19)

I am still amazed at how God has worked things out for me. When faced with challenges now, I continue to pray and believe that I will come out of the situation better than I was before. I no longer focus on how I'm going to get through it, I trust that I will.

Proverbs 3:5-7 (5) Trust in the Lord with all your heart and lean not on your own understanding; (6) in all your ways submit to him and he will make your paths straight. (7) Do not be wise in your own eyes; fear the Lord and shun evil.

I often think back to the day a pastor from the church that I served, ministered to me during the time that I was struggling with anxiety over my divorce. He told me that he could envision me helping women who were facing divorce. I didn't see it possible being that I was shy and kept to myself most of the time.

"Jesus looked at them intently and said, "Humanly speaking, it is impossible. But with God everything is possible." (Matthew 19:26)

Within two years, women facing divorce started coming to me with their stories and seeking advice. I was honored that they entrusted me, and I found fulfillment in helping them. Now, I have been granted opportunities and platforms to help women facing divorce. I went from depressed due to divorce, to finding my destiny as a spiritual leader for women facing divorce. This experience taught me that through faith and hard work, you can be an overcomer and find your destiny.

From Weighted to Waisted

Rickkita Edwards

As my story begins, I was molested at nine years old. Yes, I had the hell beat out of me almost every day starting at 18-years-old, and I disliked my body because of the Trauma, especially the image he verbally beat in my mind about my body. Being called a fat whore every day can emotionally wreck you and your self-esteem. Emotional eating is a coping mechanism, it fills the void, which causes you to overeat.

Who is he? He was an ex, and he was both physically and mentally abusive. I will not use this space to discuss the abuse I endured, you can read about that in my book *He Beat The Hell Out Of Me*. I will use this space to explain overcoming being an emotional eater and walking into my purpose!

From the Cradle to Cravings

I was six pounds, eight ounces at birth, the structure of my mother's body after 14 pregnancies (7 stillbirth - 7 survived)), would suggest my genetic makeup. In some cases, that's not necessarily true. Although your body structure is DNA, your overall body weight is based upon food consumption. At nine years old, I was average weight for a 5th grader, it wasn't until the molestation happened, which took me to a place of self-hate and that's when it seemed as though I started gaining weight rapidly. I was so withdrawn, nothing comforted me like food.

By the time I was 13, I had gained 40 pounds. My parents noticed my weight gain, but they never asked the proper questions and that caused me to sink deeper into despair. As a middle child, I was often ignored, but I found creative ways to get attention and eating had become a resource of my creativity. I was now 15 years old, 165 pounds, and acting out of rebellion. The emotional roller coaster seemed like an endless ride on the longest journey ever!

The traumatic experience made me feel unsafe in my own body. It was constantly heavy on my mind. Here I am 15 years old, holding on to a secret that happened to me at nine and then I met an older guy whose manipulation caused me to believe I could trust him with my life. A product of being molested, I'm young, I'm vulnerable, I'm naive and I'm overweight. After marrying at 18, I gained an additional 100 plus pounds, the physical and mental abuse did another number on me.

My emotional eating contributed to my massive weight gain. I was sitting over 200 pounds on a 5'1' frame. I was obese, had a bad back and knees, couldn't breathe, miserable, and I was becoming bitter. Yes, ladies, being obese will make you bitter! You will side-eye that fit chick and become guilty because you ate fried chicken with fries and she ate a salad. Emotion is tied to that bitterness- trust me! Being unhappy with your own body will cause you to lash out or feel a certain way about others. Admitting your bitterness is a step in the right direction!

I hated taking pictures, I rarely looked in the mirror. I was pretending to be happy on the outside, but it was turmoil on the inside. I wanted to be thinner. I wished for a slimmer body. I honestly cried every time I put on an outfit and it didn't fit me the way I visualized it to fit. I would get mad at myself, and I would become emotional and say forget it. He's right, I am a fat cow!

Molestation To Domestic -Manipulating- To Mastering my Mind

This gave leverage for me to throw myself into a sea of self-hatred. As I sank deeper and deeper, I felt the weight of my abusers filling my lungs, I was literally choking off of being molested and my ex's opinions of me, I almost surrendered until the lifeguard of my mother's prayers pulled me out of my despair. I came up fighting and gasping for air. I wanted to live. I needed to be free. I needed to survive. I needed to overcome it!

I knew I had to take control, control of my mind, control of the way I thought about myself. I needed to control my emotions and the way I thought about food. Food becomes a drug and if you're not careful, then you become a food addict. It's like any other addiction except it's worse. You become prone to overeating, you use food to make you feel better and emotional eating only makes you feel worse. Once you've overindulged, guess what? The problem still remains.

Emotional eating is a way to suppress feelings of anger, stress, boredom, and loneliness. You're using food to make yourself feel better, but what about the guilt? Researchers think guilt involves chemicals in your brain and how you perceive, crave, and enjoy certain foods. One study found that people who are emotional eaters have felt shame and negative self-worth. After reading that in a book, I began to recognize myself as an emotional eater. Emotional eating is a difficult cycle, but it can be broken.

My 10 Steps to Getting Waisted

1. I addressed the trauma. I became aware of the negative thoughts towards myself. I addressed the psychological aspect of hunger, (stress, anger, boredom, depression). I started focusing on the positive things in my life.

2. I started becoming sensitive to what caused my emotional triggers (a trigger is a situation that causes a painful emotion), and I started challenging those negative feelings, that's when the power of the cycle began to break. I started reading books on the power of change. I needed freedom in the area of my obesity. I didn't want food to boss me around anymore. I was the boss of my body and it was time to step up and take control of my temple.

3. Don't be afraid to get a gym membership. This is when "The Fit Females" became my friends. You will definitely need a good support system. I used the information that they gave me, and I maximized it times 10. If you don't want to join a gym, then create your in-home workout space. When you need fresh air, start walking! I started walking five miles every day. I went from walking five miles to running five miles! On the days when the weather wouldn't allow me to walk or run, I would workout at home or go to the gym and workout with the "Fit Females."

4. I understood the mentality of running my own race. I was so passionate about my pursuit of getting "waisted," and that's when the weight started falling off. Before I knew it, I was down 50 pounds. I was also cognitively not becoming a victim of the scale; the scale will depress you. A woman's body fluctuates as a result of water retention, hormone changes, and monthly cycles. I was only

weighing myself for the most accurate result and that was roughly once a month.

5. Meal prepping is your best friend. Prepping your healthy meals in advance frees up the stress of eating junk foods. This is key to reaching your fitness goals, saving money, and helping with portion control. Meal prepping will help you gain more determination and self-confidence once you see that waistline shrink.

6. I had to learn that what you eat in private, it will show in public. If you are eating poorly and exercising aggressively, then you cannot expect to see major results. Be honest with what you're eating, you will never out exercise a horrible diet! When you burn more calories than you consume, you will get your BEST RESULTS. Drink the recommended amount of water, eat lean cuts of meat, lots of green leafy vegetables, whole grains, and learn the difference between good and bad carbs.

All of these strategies are beneficial to you getting waisted.

7. Lose the EXCUSES! You will never get waisted, until you lose the excuses. Yes, ladies, we can have a ton of excuses - My hair, my feet, my back, my pinky finger, I can't do that exercise...blah blah blah. It's mind over matter or stay fatter! You choose, which one will help you reach your goals, old habits, or new workouts? Getting in shape is psychological, you have to deal with your emotions and change your behavior. Discipline, willpower, and motivation work hand-in-hand, developing good habits keeps you mentally, emotionally, and physically in shape.

8. Renew your mind daily. Read fitness magazines, get a visual picture in your mind of how you want your body to look. Speak body positive affirmations day in and day out. I remember doing a vision board and putting pictures of famous people whose bodies I admired on the board. This board was kept in a place where I saw it every day, it was motivation for me!

9. Set those goals. Get a weight loss journal, write the vision, and make it plain. I gave myself one year to lose 100 pounds. Did I want to give up? Of course, I did! Did I regress and go back to eating unhealthy food? Of course, I did! But did I quit trying? Absolutely not! Setting fitness goals holds you accountable and encourages you to keep pushing towards your goal. At any point in your fitness journey that you feel as if you've exhausted every option and you can't do it by yourself, hire a Certified Personal Trainer. -Remember - All trainers aren't created equal, so do your research and find one that will compliment your personality and your fitness goals!

10. Don't forget to celebrate the small wins as well as the big wins? I had to retrain my brain to celebrate the best measure of progress: Having more energy, feeling better on the inside, looking better on the outside. Going through life not using an inhaler or complaining about my knees or back hurting. My doctor eventually took me off of all the medications I previously had to take. I became the change I wanted to see.

Weighted Long Enough

This was huge for me to finally be able to run. It made me believe that I could do anything. I was introduced to weightlifting by a trainer that I'd hired. Losing the next 50 pounds required hard work, consistency, and discipline. By the grace of God, He allowed me to push until I reached my goal. You don't understand how high my confidence became and I wanted more. I was driven to do more.

It was the best feeling in the world to do it within the time frame that I gave myself. After losing 100 pounds, I was amazed I could wear single digits. I was extremely proud of myself, not to mention I made the ex-regret the day he ever called me fat.

I wasn't afraid to take pictures anymore. This NEW BODY didn't happen without a PLAN! It was EMPOWERING to look in the mirror and not see the verbal abuse about my weight plastered on the mirror. People started noticing my weight loss and asking if I would help them lose weight. At that time, I wasn't aware of my purpose, but I would help as many people as my time would allow and I did it Pro-Bono.

That's when my passion intensified, and I knew it was God-given. I knew it was my purpose. I just knew that God had chosen this path for me. God began to position me around some amazing trainers, people who encouraged me as well as mentored me. It was clearly time for me to walk into my fitness destiny.

I became a CPT, Owner/CEO of Waisted By Rickkita, A specialist in Exercise Therapy and I am currently working on a degree in Exercise Science.

ABOUT THE AUTHORS

Ayanna Mills Ambrose, M.B.A.

Ayanna Ambrose is a Literary Strategist that Maximizes Success. Demonstratively known as a production leader and strategic marketer in the corporate world, she now has the same reputation in the publishing industry as she applies key principles to an unmatched proven track record.

Ayanna is also an Evangelist and a #1 Best Selling Author of Non-fiction Transformational books. As a first-year author, she wrote and compiled 10 bestselling books in 10 months. Ayanna's books are not just bestselling in the United States, where she lives, but also in the United Kingdom, Canada, France, and India.

Ayanna uses her strong literary skills as a facilitator at Bestselling Authors University, a school she founded to teach aspiring authors, independent authors, and goal-getters to write, market, and publish bestselling books.

Ayanna also reconnected with her high school sweetheart and is newly married. She resides with her husband, 3 sons, and dog Cupid in Alpharetta, Georgia, USA. Ayanna can be found at https://thanxamills.com/ or https://bestsellingauthorsuniversity.teachable.com and ceo@thanxamills.com.

Beatrice N. Charles

Beatrice Charles comes from a stream of resilient women. Born in Haiti to a then newly widowed mother. Three years later, her mother fled the country to give her a better life. Beatrice migrated to the United States five years later at the tender age of 8. Beatrice has a background in hospitality management and is a serial entrepreneur, who loves creating generational wealth and building a legacy for her 2 children. Zachary, her Sunshine as she affectionately calls him and daughter Olivia Grace, known as (Livi Lou) ages 18 and 13. Beatrice has a passion for mentoring young girls and broken women. Her heart is especially for single mothers. She prides herself in sharing her story with transparency and authenticity in hopes of healing and impacting every life she is privileged to touch. Beatrice is a motivational speaker and women's empowerment coach. As a trauma survivor, she rebuilt her life by working God's Word and reclaiming her joy. She is committed to helping you transform your pain into PURPOSE.

Blanca Solorzano

Blanca Solorzano was born in El Salvador, Central America and at the age of 4 she moved to Freeport, NY, where she grew up and graduated from Freeport High School. Blanca graduated from high school with honors and went on to Boston University on an academic scholarship then transferred to SUNY Stony Brook University.

While at school she fell in love with her soulmate and decided to start a family. In order to not give up on her education she went back to school and obtained her Paralegal Studies Degree. For the past 15 years, Blanca has gained professional status as a paralegal trained in assisting attorneys in the field of personal injury.

Besides her career, Blanca enjoys being a part of her community and has served on parent committees for her son's sports teams and served in other community groups in soup kitchens and toy drives. In addition, she served as Secretary for two years on the Board of Directors for H.E.L.P. Services, which is an organization for youth, family, and substance abuse services.

Currently, Blanca lives a humble life on Long Island, NY with her spouse, Rafael of 21 years and her two wonderful children, Isaiah who is 18 and Ashlyn who is 5 years old. Motherhood has been an important part of her life and Blanca prides herself in teaching her children that like her first love, music, a song is an inspiration of your life's journey. It is poetically an expression of a story only you can tell and show the world.

Dr. Anu Binny

Dr. Anu Binny holds a doctorate in Engineering. She is a TEDx Speaker, International Trainer, and Designing Your Life Coach. She was born and raised in India in a middle-class family. Her journey from a broke mother to a successful first-generation woman entrepreneur is inspirational. She draws on her own experience of struggling with patriarchy, domestic violence, single mom, self-identity issues, introverted nature, multiple setbacks, and how she worked her way up the corporate ladder and achieved success both personally and professionally. She has won many awards to her credit and is also invited as a Speaker for her subject knowledge and motivation. She believes everyone deserves to thrive and conducts workshops to inspire and empower anyone who is contemplating a whole new future. She helps clients with the tools and step-by-step guide to leaving their failures behind, better understand themselves and create a life that will work for them. She has a special heart for introverts and people who have faced a setback.

She is an avid lover of Indian handicraft and loves to travel the length and breadth of India visiting historical places to know more about her land and its inspiring culture. To know more about her life, her work and speaking engagements visit her website https://Anubinny.com or connect@anubinny. com

Dr. Margarita David

Dr. Margarita David is a bilingual, doctorally-prepared registered nurse and founder of the Dr. Registered Nurse Success Academy, LLC. a company that provides mentoring and consulting services to prospective nurses and corporate professionals and guides doctoral students throughout their entire doctoral journey. Dr. David also holds a Bachelor's in Business Management & Administration with a Minor in Economics, Bachelor's in Nursing, and a Master's in Nursing Education and Leadership. In addition to helping students on a 1-1 basis, Dr. David helps aspiring nurses thrive as a Clinical Adjunct Professor, and via her YouTube channel "Dr. Registered Nurse," where she provides easy-to-comprehend nursing content videos of hard-to-understand concepts. Dr. David was born in the Dominican Republic and immigrated to the United States at the age of six where she lived in the Bronx, NY for most of her childhood and early adult years, is a wife of over 20 years, and a mom of 3.

Dr. Merary Simeon

Dr. Merary Simeon is a wife, mother, co-founder of Color Forward podcast, founder of the ACTivate Conference, board member, ministry volunteer, and proven Human Resources Executive with more than 20 years of experience working for various Fortune 100 companies. Merary's diverse experiences have equipped her with a deep understanding of the needs and opportunities critical to leaders. Her leadership expertise includes Diversity & Inclusion, Talent

Management, Leadership Consulting, Culture Change, Executive Coaching, and Public Speaking.

Merary holds a doctorate in strategic leadership from Regent University and has a master's degree in Human Resources from Fordham University.

She is a native of Puerto Rico and currently resides in Frisco, Texas, with her family. She credits her success to Jesus Christ. *"I can do all things through Christ who gives me strength,"* Philippians 4:13.

Erica Nobles

Erica Nobles is a small-town girl with dreams to change the world. To be a ray of light in the dark. She has worked for Fortune 500 companies in a customer centric capacity and helped others promote and grow their businesses. She is now preparing to launch her own business. She has been a "Jack of all Trades for everyone else but has now chosen to focus on being the master of her own for herself." Erica currently lives in the Atlanta, Georgia area with her son. She is a mother, daughter, sister, aunt and friend. She wants to see everyone rise above their circumstances and any restrictions placed on them by others. She wants them to intentionally walk into their true destiny. She has a passion to see people succeed, especially to those whom the world says cannot or should not.

Felicia Butler

Felicia Butler is a Nurse Practitioner, Online Instructor, Nursing Preceptor, Travel Agent, Life Insurance Agent and a Work at Home entrepreneur. She was born in Spain, has lived in Germany, but raised in Columbia, Missouri. She received a Bachelor of Science degree in Nursing in 1988 from the University of Missouri-Columbia. In 2006, she received a Master of Science degree in Nursing from Maryville University-St. Louis, and practices as an Adult Nurse Practitioner in an Occupational Health clinic in St. Louis, Missouri. She is married and has three grown children and five grown step-children. She has worked in the healthcare industry for over 30 years. Her accomplishments outside of her educational achievements include, creating a medical mobile app for commercial drivers, and organizing a free wellness center for the underserved. She is a member of the Sigma Theta Tau, American Nurses Association, Missouri Nurses Association, University of Missouri Alumni Association, and is board certified by the American Nurses Association of Nurse Practitioners.

Katina Walker

Katina Walker is a Licensed Insurance advisor and Risk Management Analyst. She previously served in the Army as a Logistics Specialist. Her company Katwalk Consulting was established to help divorced, single moms, like herself, establish financial security as well as build nest eggs for their children's future. She studied English at Georgia State University and Grand Canyon University.

Born and raised in Georgia, Katina currently resides in the Metro Atlanta Area with her daughter, who is her only child. She and her daughter volunteer their time and resources to Restoring One's Hope of Atlanta, an organization that feeds the homeless. She enjoys nature watching and attending Auto shows. Katina can be found on Instagram and Facebook at Katwalk629 and Katina Walker.

Orjanette Bryant

Orjanette Butler is a 6-time published author, public speaker, a mother of three children, a hospitalist nurse practitioner, an IV business owner, and financial literacy consultant. Her passion is teaching and supporting others. Bryant transitioned her researched knowledge of a chemical free approach to hair care into her first publication Nubia's Guide to Going Natural. Her second publication collaboration Small Voices Heard- The Parental Guide which was rated a 4/5 by the Reader's Digest.

Mrs. Bryant turned her life as a troubled teenager into a mission of hope. She leans to God to overcome as she cares for others. Through giving to various community organizations and supporting the youth she was nominated for the Live your Dream Award by the Soroptimist International of greater Daytona Beach in 2017.

Rickkita Edwards

Rickkita Edwards is an entrepreneur, author, and motivational speaker. In 2006, after overcoming her own struggles she founded WaistedbyRickkita to help countless others transform by taking control of their lives and becoming who they were meant to be. Her mission to help others was born out of her ability to successfully transform her life by losing over 100 pounds. She took what she learned and built on her knowledge and experience by becoming a Certified Personal Trainer and a Certified Exercise Therapy Specialist evolving into a lifestyle change rooted in her ability to help others achieve results.

During the incredible circumstances we all faced in 2020, Rickkita, continued to expand her ability to support clients by shifting her work to a virtual platform. She continues to expand her growth as demonstrated when she authored a life-changing debut autobiography about her journey to regain self-love. *He Beat the Hell Out of Me - From Doormat to Destiny*, details how she was able to rise from victim to victor by surviving an abusive relationship and evolving into the incredibly strong and courageous woman she is today. Rickkita uses her experience and voice to empower others to find their voices by turning their pain into purpose through mentoring and motivational speaking engagements.

Tammy Lyons

Tammy Lyons is an author, lawyer, and movie producer. She resides in California. The focus of her legal career has been to help others who cannot help themselves. She underwent a spiritual transformation during a turbulent time in her life. During her spiritual journey, she has become a certified hypnotist and Reiki Master. She took classes at Chicago School of Psychology to better understand the world around her. Helping individuals reach their full potential is her focus in life. She mentor's college students assisting them in the transition from high school to college then on to a rewarding career.

Tammy has overcome many obstacles in her own personal life and uses that information to transform others around. She inspires others with her daily encouragement. She has coached others transforming their lives into one filled with joy and purpose. Her goal is to leave a positive impact on everyone she meets. She follows the philosophy that one kind word can transform a person.

When not encouraging others, she is constantly traveling, walking the world, and inspiring others. She has traveled from Mexico to Turkey and beyond the Great Wall of China leaving her mark on the world. Her goal is to reach out to more people through speaking engagements and her inspirational writings.

Tarsha N. Howard, MPA

Tarsha Howard, native resident of Brooklyn, New York is a loving mom and enjoys guiding her son Joshua on the path of life. She is a Born Again Christian and applies Biblical principles to solve real-life problems. For self-development, Tarsha has committed her life to ongoing learning and training. In the marketplace, Tarsha is a Certified Legal Support Professional and has supported attorneys in large and midsize law firms. Her niche is in the Intellectual Property practice. As a part-time Kingdom Entrepreneur, Tarsha formulates organic beauty care products. She is the owner of a small organic beauty care company called PrettyOrganix, LLC.

Teresa Moreno

Teresa Moreno is CEO and Founder of Roma Business Services, Inc., a company that provides business owners and entrepreneurs opportunities and access to systems to generate multiple streams of income to create financial freedom, build generational wealth and leave an abundant legacy. She is an advocate for single moms and empowers them to become financially self-sufficient. For the past 14 years, she has successfully owned and operated small businesses and has participated in product and service-based companies, team development training and personal coaching.

Raised in Los Angeles, CA. Teresa received a Bachelor of Arts degree in Social Work from California State University, Los Angeles. As a community leader, she leads workshops on financial literacy and personal and business growth and development. When she is not writing, she invests her time learning, reading, creating new business with her kids and exploring her creative side.

Keep in touch with Teresa online at www.teresa-moreno.com and on social platforms Facebook @facebook.com/teresamoreno, Instagram @burdie2224, on clubhouse @teresamoreno

Tonya Kent

Tonya Kent is a mother of four beautiful children and the grandmother of nine loving grandchildren. She currently resides in Colorado Springs. Tonya, a woman of faith, integrity, and virtue, was once a woman in bondage to substance abuse, codependency, guilt, fear, shame, and illiteracy. "I now see myself as a woman of God with a mission to see other women set free - free of the cycles of abuse, depression, suicide, poverty, illiterate, and dysfunctional relationships that once controlled my life."

Tonya has earned three degrees at Solano Community College, one in Human Services (AA), the other in University Studies: Social Science (AA), and lastly, University Studies: Liberal Studies (AA). In Summer of 2017, Tonya graduated from the University of California at Davis with a B.A. in African American Studies. Besides, I graduated in November 2019 from JEZREEL School of Theology. Lastly, Tonya graduated in December 2019 from John Franklin Kennedy Law School, Pleasant Hill, with a Paralegal Certificate.

Made in the USA
Monee, IL
20 May 2021